BUREAUCRACY AND DEVELOPMENT IN MEGHALAYA

BUREAUCRACY AND DEVELOPMENT IN MEGHALAYA

DEBASISH BHATTACHARJEE

With a Foreword by
Dr. B.D. Sharma
Vice-Chancellor
North Eastern Hill University
Shillong

UPPAL PUBLISHING HOUSE
NEW DELHI-110002

UPPAL PUBLISHING HOUSE
3, Ansari Road, Daryaganj, New Delhi-110002

ISBN 81-85024-01-4

Printed in India
Published by B.S. Uppal, Uppal Publishing House, Daryaganj, New Delhi-110002, and Printed by Latika Printers, Maujpur, Shahdara, Delhi-110053.

DEDICATED
TO
MY PARENTS

Foreword

The basic frame of our administration was designed and firmly established during the colonial period incorporating many elements of the Moghul system. The main objective of administration during the British period was to maintain law and order, to dispense justice in accordance with the new formal system and to become a symbol of British power in India. While the lower ranks of the administrative system were manned by a new class of Indians educated in English schools, the personnel for higher services was mostly drawn initially from the home country which was gradually Indianised. In course of time, a number of services were organised for undertaking a set of comparable functions in administration in each case. The system was heirarchical and headed by an elite group of the Indian Civil Service which came to be known as the steel frame of British administration in India. Even as functional specilisation continued to grow, the members of the Indian Civil Service were expected to provide the leadership, assume any responsibility which came in their way or was expected of them in any situation and keep up the tradition of their service as a peer group of loyalty, honesty, objectivity, efficiency and direct contact to the people.

The legal administrative structure so established was a fine rational conduct balancing powers with responsibility with built-in provision for full discretion to meet unusual situations in a vast country with varying conditions—social, economic and political. Even though comprehensive laws were enacted, rules formulated and procedures prescribed, the action of individuals in the field was supported notwithstanding the fact that the abberations were also meticulously noted and commented upon. This gave the man on the spot a sense of confidence and responsibility and the services in the field became the bulwark of administration. The system had a tremendous resilience which is even now exemplified in effective handling of crisis situation by the administration.

With the dawn of independence, the state assumed a new role in our country as the establishment of an egalitarian society was accepted as the national goal in the constitution by the founding fathers. The services gave an excellent account of their inherent strength to meet the crisis situation on many fronts beginning with the aftermath of partition. Nevertheless, as situation stabilised and the country settled to undertake the serious task of building up its economy, the need for a new administrative system and melieu and a different orientation for the administrators became increasingly clear. The Indian administration no doubt took up the task assigned to it, but a variety of issues in a number of areas like the relationship between the administration and the political leadership, the quality of interaction between the administration and the people, inter-services relationships, commitments versus neutrality in administration, the guiding principles for operation of the system itself, etc. came to the fore. While in principle, there is general consensus on most of these issues, in effect the change has not been in keeping with the demands of the emerging situations.

The administrative organisations have grown phenomenally both in the Centre and in the States. A large number of institutions had to be established for assuming new responsibilities of developing administration, but a large mass of doubtful value has also been gathered ostensibly in the name of specialisation as also to provide for larger employment opportunities. The real motive appears to have been the leverage which such expansion can provide to those in authority. In the new situation where the roles and responsibilities of different partners in the system became rather blurred and remain to be accepted in the true spirit, many anomalies have arisen. For example, while the policy making should be a prerogative of the political executive, and the details of administration the responsibility of the system, the roles appeared to have been the reverse. The details of administration, relating not only to development programmes, which should be guided by a national planning frame, but also about postings and transfers, appointments in subordinate organisations, etc. have become the primary pre-occupations of the political executive, which is largely under public pressure but the lure of visible authority inherent in such decisions has also played a major role. Similarly, policy decisions in a democratic setup must be made in rational frame; a rational decision can provide great personal satisfaction. Yet in can hardly be used for personal glorification in the immediate context. These deviations have caused a great strain on the public administration of the country, and rationality, objectivity and anonymity, the three essential elements of a competent bureaucratic system needed for effective implementation, are at a great discount.

Even the public administration itself has not been able to keep a balance between the invisible essentials of the system and the visible that is glorious which can be only a small part of the total reality. If all parts of an administrative system function smoothly requiring no external effort, it is taken for granted like the air for life which has no economic value. Most facets of general administration and even a large part of development administration falls in this category. Some facets of development, administration, however, are in the visible category. It is unfortunate that the invisible essentials have been rather neglected to the detriment of the entire development process. That peace and order are the essential infrastructure for economic development is now being acutely realised, though rather belatedly as nothing seems to work where law and order situation has deteriorated beyond a point. That 95% of public administration is sheer drudgery and its application to mundane details does not seem to be fully appreciated by either the system or the individual administrators. Consequently, there is a rat race for those positions in the system, which either bring visibility, or have a lot of discretion relating to those sections of the society, which make for that visibility, and create an aura around individuals. The significance of the funcitional roles, therefore is lost. This malice is permeating the entire system and erupts in the form of inter-personnel, inter-sectional and inter-service rivalries. The members of the bureaucratic system and services which comprise positions with comparable job requirements recede in the background and those who occupy the glamorous positions are always locked in rivalry. This is at the base of protracted controversy between what are known as the generalist services and the specialist services. While the rationale of a small service which is constituted on broad-based generalist principles is questioned, yet the controversy subsides the moment the various pressure groups are able to get a share in what are supposed to be the coveted positions notwithstanding the fact that the resultant situation is devoid even of the questionable rationality of a specially trained generalist service yielding to 'generalist principle with vengeance' where anyone with whatever background can stake a claim to any position in the system, unless it is included in a formally recognised technical group requiring qualifications like medicines, engineering and such like. That the public administration itself is a speciality, in which skill is acquired on the job rather than in formal academic institutions, has by and large not adequately been appreciated so far.

The other important issue is the so called neutrality and commitment in civil service. No system can afford to be neutral in a dynamic situation even, for example, in the limited sphere of law and order. When there is a clash the first task undoubtedly is to restore peace and book the guilty. But unless the administrator goes to the root cause of the clash, no lasting peace is possible and justice in the real sense of the term would not have been meted out. When we come to the great task of economic development, the perceptions of the people manning the administrative system becomes crucial. It is best illustrated in relation to the central issue of land reforms and land to the tiller in the post-independence period. Unfortunately, the administrative system happened to be in sympathy with the bigger landholders, and not much progress has been made notwithstanding a series of legislations.

Our administration has not been able to make a common cause with the large masses of people in the country : this is becoming clearer as the dualistic structure is consolidating and vulgar affluence stares defiantly at our face, while stark poverty remains the fate of countless millions.

Shri Debasish Bhattacharjee has undertaken a considerable indepth study of development and administration in Meghalaya, which throws valuable light on many of the issues facing public administration in the country as a whole. Like elsewhere the controversy between the generalist administrative services and specialist services continues to be raised which is affecting the morale of the services badly. An unusual feature of Meghalaya situation is the feeling of insider and outsider, notwithstanding the fact that the Indian Administrative Service is known to have been consciously designed to draw upon the talent from all over the country and to give a mixed character to it in each state. All sections of administrators, generalists and specialists, in Meghalaya appear to be satisfied with the status and prestige they enjoy, but the strains due to inflation are visible almost everywhere equally. That the number of engineering and even medical services should have a low level of job satisfaction needs serious consideration and deeper probe both in the structure of the services as also the tasks assigned to these professional groups.

That the administration in Meghalaya is under pressure from the political system as anywhere else has been clearly brought out in the study. The causes which lead to corruption are well known once. An important finding of the study is the divergence between the value frame in the constitution and the perceptions of the members of various services. The difference is significant on issues like secularism, equality and democracy. The findings on the last two points are rather surprising. A large section of the members of the administrative and technical services belong to the tribal communities who have a strong tradition of egalitarian democratic structure at the village level. Nevertheless a little reflection helps to explain since most of the civil servants hail from the urban areas and have lost their traditional rural moorings.

Another important finding of the study is the divergence between the needs of the area in terms of development programmes and the perceptions of the civil servants in relation thereto. With vast dormant natural resources in the region, at the present stage, only a major thrust in the primary sector can help in establishing the strong foundation for its economic development. It is surprising that most of the civil servants feel that industrialisation is the answer to the complex economic problems of the region and agriculture does not deserve a high priority. This is really a reflection of the national ethos in which industrialisation has acquired mythical character and has been accepted as holding the key of development in the national economy. It is high time that this myth is exploded and the civil servants, who are responsible for advising the political executive on policy formulation and preparing the blueprints for development and their implementation, are suitably re-oriented.

Vice-Chancellor, **Dr. B. D. Sharma**
November 10, 1985. North-Eastern Hill University
Shillong-793001

Preface

It is increasingly recognised that much of the success of our development programmes depends upon the effective performance of bureaucracy. Bureaucracy is now considered to be the principal instrument of nation-building and development. But over the years, the shortfalls in bureaucratic performance in India have proved to be a major obstacle to development. The general public, scholars and leaders of public opinion are unanimous in their evaluation of our administrative organisation as being ineffective and ill-equipped for massive tasks of nation-building and socio-economic development. But why has the bureacuracy failed in its task of nation-building and development ?

In this study, an attempt has been made to answer this question with particular reference to the higher bureaucracy in Meghalaya. The scope of the study has been restricted to the higher bureacuracy because it is this managerial group which is more likely to have a direct bearing on political, economic and other kinds of development. The perspective informing this study does not treat bureaucracy as a conglomeration of rules, regulations and precedents. It emphasises the interaction pattern of bureaucracy with its environment as well as some of its behavioural features in order to highlight the problems that the bureaucracy faces in the performance of its role as a major instrument of development in Meghalaya. In this sense, this study is a departure from conventional studies in the field of public administration.

However, Meghalaya being a newly created state, there is not much of documentary and published material on the functioning of bureaucracy in the state. Hence, I had to spend considerable time at various departments of the government to collect material for the present study and to know their working, practices and problems through discussions with officials belonging to different classes and grades. Secondly, I issued a questionnaire to the Civil Servants of different services and grades. Their answers to the questionnaire form the basis of analysis and discussion of problems in a major part of the book. An analysis of their responses to different questions is given in the respective chapters and appropriate places. The qustionnaires has been reproduced in an appendix to this book. The third was the documentary source and consisted of various reports and research publications.

Silchar
April 14, 1985

Debasish Bhattacharjee
Department of Political Science,
Cachar College, Silchar.

Acknowledgements

I am indebted to Dr. C. N. Bhalerao, Professor and formerly Head, Department of Political Science, North-Eastern Hill University, Shillong, for initiating me into the field of behavioural studies in administration and for his inspiring guidance at all the stages of my studies. It was due to his encouragement that I undertook this study for my Ph.D. degree as a UGC Research Fellow. He provided a perspective and a direction to my study. I am grateful to Dr. B. D. Sharma, Vice-Chancellor, North-Eastern Hill University, Shillong, for having agreed to write the foreword. I am also grateful to Dr. R. L. Walli, formerly Head, Department of Political Science, North-Eastern Hill University, Shillong, for his encouragement and valuable suggestions that I received at all stages of my studies.

The study owes a great deal of encouragement from Sri Ramesh Chandra, I.A.S., formerly Chief Secretary to the Government of Meghalaya and Dr. Dhruba Das, I.A.S., Deputy Commissioner, Jaintia Hills District. I am very much thankful to them for the stimulating discussions I had with them on various problems of my study and for exploring fruitful lines of enquiry. I also benefited greatly from discussions with Mrs. M.R. Mawlong, A.C.S., formerly Registrar of the North-Eastern Hill University and now, the D.P.I., Government of Meghalaya and Mr. A.K. Roy, M.C.S., Deputy Secretary to the Government of Meghalaya. My thanks go as well to Mr. Smiling War and other officials of the Department of Personnel and Administrative Reforms, Government of Meghalaya, for their help in the collection of data regarding the bureaucratic organisation in Meghalaya. I also express my deep sense of gratitude to the various civil servants of the Government of Meghalaya who desire to remain anonymous here, for their encouragement and cooperation without which this study could not have been completed.

I am also indebted to my colleagues, especially to Sri Apurbananda Majumdar and Sri Jyotilal Choudhury of Cachar College, Silchar, for sparing their valuable time to go through the manuscript and offer me valuable suggestion.

I acknowledge my thanks to University Grants Commission, New-Delhi, for awarding me a Research Fellowship to undertake the present study.

I am thankful to Sri Dhiraj Chakraborty of the Department of Political Science, North-Eastern Hill University, Shillong, for typing out the manuscripts under most difficult condition.

I also take this opportunity so thank Sri B.S. Uppal of Uppal Publishing House for the prompt and efficient publication of this volume.

Cachar College
SILCHAR.

Debsish Bhattacharjee

Contents

1

Introduction

The developing countries are committed to the twin goals of nation-building and socio-economic development. This commitment to the goals of nation-building and socio-economic development involves a rapid and sustained change both on social and economic fronts. Changes in the developing countries are basic and large-scale and are sought to be brought about within a short period of time. This underlines the immensity of the task that the developing countries are facing. They have to come out of their traditional social and cultural moorings and have to accommodate their traditional values, attitudes and institutions to the demands of social and economic change. They have to widen the people's participation in political process and developmental programmes They have also to create new opportunities and to enlarge the range of distribution of economic benefits so as to satisfy the people's aspirations for upward mobility. As S.J. Eldersveld, A.P. Barnabas and V. Jagannadham observe, the problem confronting the developing countries "is to accommodate the past with the modern present, to economize resources in the face of mounting and cumulating crises, and to elicit intelligent and meaningful co-operation from a public thus far ignorant and indifferent in its orientations towards the distant government".[1] All these problems need to be grappled with and solved simultaneously to bring about desired changes for the development of the country.

In this task, the government has to play a crucial role in planning, initiating and executing developmental programmes and activities. It has to function not only as the 'prime energizer' of development efforts but also as an agent of change. In acting as an agent of change what the government needs more is the public co-operation without which a well-conceived plan of development is likely to become ineffective. The public co-operation in the nation building activities depends upon three factors: (1) "the degree of value-congruence between the modernising elites and the mass of citizens; (2) effectiveness of the political sector in problem-solving; and (3) the extent of structural shift in the distribution of political power".[2]

The above mentioned three factors are the conditions necessary for getting support for a political system. But, what are the structures which can effectively mobilise such support? There are two structures for mobilising support, i.e., the "administrative system" and "political leadership."[3] Between the two structures, the bureaucratic structure is more important than the political structure because it has firm roots in developing countries. "While political leadership, party organisation, the electoral system, and elected legislatures all

1. S.J. Eldersveld, A.P. Barnabas, and V. Jagannadhan, *The Citizen and the Administrator in a Developing Democracy : An Empirical Study in Delhi State,* (New-Delhi : The Indian Institute of Public Administration, 1968), p. 2.

2. Shanti Kothari and Ramashray Roy, *Relations between Politicians and Administrators at the District Level* (New-Delhi: Indian Institute of Public Administration and the Centre of Applied Politics, 1969), p.5.

3. *Ibid.*, p.6.

are in a state of flux, bureaucracy continues to provide permanent leadership in the administration of developing societies."[4] In contrast to the political structures, the bureaucratic structures of government are well institutionalised and show stability and continuity. Consequently, developmental efforts have to rely heavily on bureaucratic structure.

Bureaucracy in India

Before we formulate any specific issue for discussion, it will be worthwhile to provide a historical perspective of administration in India which will help us in understanding the impact of historical forces on the present bureaucratic system.

Bureaucracy, as we understand to-day, did not exist in India before the advent of the British rule. It was the British who laid the foundation of modern bureaucracy in India, a bureaucracy based on rules, well defined authority, integrated hierarchical structure, and merit and open competition. The British period is characterised by unification of the subcontinent and the establishment of a single political rule which became possible through an elaborate and integrated administrative system. Based on the district pattern of the Moghuls, a hierarchical structure of administration was established from the centre downward with the provinces and districts acting as the subordinate agencies.[5] The basic Moghul structure of district administration was retained but was strengthened by converting it into modern bureaucratic organisation.

Initially, the Britishers came to India for trading purpose. But gradually, the company began to acquire territorial

4. C.P. Bhambri, *Administrators in a Changing Society* (First ed., Delhi : National Publishing House, 1972), p.17.

5. Rajni Kothari, *Politics in India*, (New-Delhi : Orient Longman Ltd., 1972), p.38.

jurisdiction and political power, culminating in the building up of the British Empire in India. At the initial stage of empire-building, the mercantile employees of the company became the administrators and the term 'Civil Service' acquired its present meaning.[6] A youngman was recruited first as an 'Apprentice', the other superior grades were those of 'Writers', 'Factors', 'Junior Merchants', and 'Senior Merchants'. In the beginning, the candidates were selected by the Court of Directors on their request or petition. But by an order of 1731 that "in future all petitions for employment in the Company's service, either at home or abroad, be presented by some gentlemen in the Direction",[7] there emerged the patronage of the Directors and the covenanted civil service virtually became the monopoly of certain families. To a considerable extent, recruitement to the Civil Service under East India Company was made from the governing classes and wealthy professional classes at home. They were paid poorly but they augmented their income by private initiative such as private dealings, maintenance of monopoly of control of new products, and collection of grafts on taxes and receipt of gifts.[8]

But as the company grew and its responsibility increased, interest of the Civil Servants ran counter to the interest of the company. In some cases, exaction on the local population led to war as well as serious financial deficit for the company. As a result of this, attempts were made to place limits on the rapacity of the Company's servants, so that by serving the company well they would also serve themselves. This was done by the Regulating Act of 1773 which made a distinction between the Civil and the Commercial functions of the

6. Biswanath Prasad, *The Indian Administrative Service*, (New Delhi : S.Chand & Co., 1968), p.11.

7. Quoted by Biswanath Prasad, *Ibid*.

8. P.L. Bansal, *Administrative Development in India*, (New Delhi : Sterling Publishers Pvt. Ltd., 1974), p.2.

company and abolished the right of private trading and acceptance of gifts by those personnel who were engaged in the civil administration of the company.[9] In 1776, salaries were raised for the first time and it was argued that mere legislation could not remove corruption unless the officials were placed above temptation which was possible only through payment of good salaries.

Towards the end of the eighteenth century, Lord Wellesley's accession to the office of the Governor-General marked the beginning of a new phase in India. His arrival ushered in the dawn of imperialism in all its dimensions. Administratively, it gave rise to the need for a strong and trained bureaucracy, an executive administration based on a combination of powers. Thus, for the purpose of making an institutional arrangement for the regular training and education of the Civil Servants, the Fort William College was established in Calcutta in 1800, which was later on replaced by the Haileybury College in England in 1805.[10] Though the opinion is divided as regards the objectives and performance of Haileybury College, its common training programme did help the Civil Servants to be efficient, honest and upright, on the one hand, and make them believe in social exclusivity, on the other. The Civil Servants "became in themselves a social class, class of aristocracy of talent, race and even of colour."[11]

The growth of imperialism and free trade also made it necessary to replace the patronage of the company through public examination. The Act of 1833 proposed the introduction

9. B.B. Misra, *Bureaucracy in India: A Historical Analysis of Development upto 1947*, (First ed., Bombay : Oxford University Press, 1977), pp. 46-47.

10. Bansal, *op. cit.*

11- *Ibid.*, p.4.

of limited competition but it did not materialise.[12] The Macaulay Committee which was appointed in 1853 to report on the subject, strongly recommended an examination that was to be on subjects of liberal education rather than on those especially more useful to Indian Civil Servants; no premium was to be held out for knowledge, wide surface and small depth.[13] On the basis of the Macaulay Committee's report, the first examination was held in 1855 and the service came to be known as the Indian Civil Service which represented the best elite from the best families of England.[14]

The Indian Civil Service was a generalist service and the I.C.S. officers could be placed in any job and was considered fit for it. "There was no department-police, forest, opium, salt, education, health—where he could not be posted".[15] The I.C.S. was the sole repository of power in Indian Society.[16] It provided good income, power and high prestige and status. The status of the I.C.S. was evident from the large amount of dowry which they could command on marriage.[17]

The I.C.S. officers occupied superior positions in the administration and were always at the top of the administrative hierarchy. The superior positions of the I.C.S. in administrative hierarchy were jealously guarded by the British, and as

12. Misra, *op.cit.*, p.65.

13. Prasad, *op.cit.*, p.14.

14. N.K. Singhi, *Bureaucracy: Positions and Persons*, (First ed., New Delhi: Abhinav Publications, 1974), p.16.

15. *Ibid.*, p.19.

16. W.H. Morris-Jones, *The Government and Politics of India*, (Bombay: B.I. Publications, 1974), p. 23.

17. Richard P. Taub, *Bureaucrats under Stress*, (Calcutta: Firma K.L. Mukhopadhyaya, 1969), p. 11.

a group, the I.C.S. became exclusive.[18] The main function of the I.C.S. was the maintenance of law and order and the collection of revenue. It was a service eminently suited for governing a colonial empire. The I.C.S. officers did not need to share their authority with any local body or assembly. Their function was to govern from above and they were neither responsible nor responsive to the people. Describing the function of the I.C .S., N.C. Roy observes :

> From the very start they (members of the I.C.S.) chose some functions as the essential duties of the government. They concentrated all their efforts upon their performance and they performed them with as much efficiency as their general education, natural ability and special training might allow. They showed their genius in particularly building up the administrative structure which had collapsed in the great anarchy. They had great achievement to their credit in making law and order and in dealing with revenue problems. Beyond these functions they were loath to look. This narrow outlook was engendered in them partly by the fact that in the nineteenth century Britain. Laissez-faire was the principle which had struck root. Secondly, being mostly Britishers, the Civil Servants were interested in the maintenance of British supremacy and not with those other functions which might administer to the welfare of the people but might also have sown seeds of dissolution of the British Empire in India.[19]

Post-Independence Period

In August, 1947, the British left the country but the administrative system they built up during their colonial period remained intact not only in its form but also in its characteristics.[20] Writing about the inadequacies of Indian

18. C.P. Bhambhri, *Bureaucracy and Politics in India,* (First ed., Delhi: Vikas Publications, 1971), p.59.

19. Quoted by Bansal, *op.cit.*, p.7.

20. Morris-Jones, *op.cit.,* p.25.

bureaucracy, Taylor, Ensminger and their associates point out that "... the inadequacies of Indian bureaucracy are not due to the fact that it is a bureaucracy but, due to a considerable extent, to the fact that it carries too much baggage from the past".[21] In fact, there has not been any significant break with the past. Of course, after independence, it was difficult for the national leaders to bring about a wholesale change in the administrative system, a system which was credited with establishing political unification of the country. The nation after independence, was confronted with many complex problems like those of the integration of the country, communal riots and the influx of a large number of refugees from both the Eastern and Western sectors of Pakistan. The law and order situation at that time was also under threat. The combination of all these factors left very little choice before the national leaders but to continue with the administrative system that was pre-eminently suited for a colonial country.

After independence, the I.A.S. occupied the place of the I.C.S. and provided top administrative personnel to the Central as well as to the State Governments. The recruitment pattern has almost remained the same following Macaulay's principles of liberal education, generalist and not specialised competitive examination, and early age recruitment. The Union Public Service Commission conducts competitive examinations every year for recruitment to Indian Administrative Service, Indian Police Service, Indian Foreign Service and other Central services while the State Public Services Commissions hold competitive examinations for recruitment to the respective State services.

The conditions of eligibility and the courses for I.A.S., etc. examinations are shown in table 1 : 1. Any Indian citizen between the age of twenty-one and twenty-six years

21. Quoted by Kuldeep Mathur, *Bureaucratic Response to Development*, (First ed., Delhi : National Publishing House, 1972), pp. 2-3.

holding a degree from a recognised College or University is eligible for the competitive examination. For the I.P.S., however, the age limit is twenty to twenty-six years. The upper age limit is relaxable by five years in case of Scheduled Castes and Scheduled Tribes candidates and eight years in special cases.

The examination (upto 1979) consists of a written test and a viva-voce. Candidates who qualify in the written test are called for interview. Until 1956, candidates who failed to secure a minimum percentage of marks in the interview were not considered eligible to enter the service, regardless of their performance in the written examination. However, at present, each part of the examination is given a numerical value. Candidates performing well in the written examination may compensate for poor performance in the interview.[22] The subjects for written examination include three compulsory papers and two optional papers for I.P.S. and three for the I.A.S. and central services. In addition, the candidates opting for the I.A.S. and I.F.S. are required to offer two advanced papers.

Women, may, however, compete only if they are unmarried. If a women marries subsequent to entering she may be asked to resign, if the maintenance of the efficiency of the service so requires.

However, following the recommendation of the Kothari Commission, the U.P.S.C. introduced certain changes in the scheme of examination since 1979.[23] Now, the commission annually holds an uniform examination called Civil Service Examinations.[24] Any Indian citizen who is a graduate from a

22. Taub, *op. cit.*, p. 29.

23. For details of the new scheme, see table 1: 2.

24. The material regarding the Civil Service Examination is collected from *Employment News* (Special Supplement) of 20th December, 1980.

recognised university and whose age is between twenty-one and twenty-eight years is eligible for the Civil Service Examinations. The upper age limit is relaxable by three to eight years in different cases.

The examination comprises two successive stages : Civil Service preliminary Examination (Objective Type) for the selection of candidates for the main examination ; and the Civil Service Main Examination (written and interview) for the selection of candidates for the various services and posts. The Preliminary Examination consists of two papers of objective type (multiple-choice questions) and carries a maximum of 450 marks. This examination is meant to serve as a screening test only, the marks obtained in the Preliminary Examination by the candidates who are declared qualified for admission to the Main Examination are not counted for determining their final order of merit. The number of candidates to the Main Examination are about ten times total approximate number of vacancies to be filled in the year in the various services and posts.

The Main Examination consists of a written examination and an interview test. The written examination consists of eight papers of conventional essay type each carrying 300 marks. However, the papers on Indian Languages and English are of qualifying nature and the marks obtained in these papers are not counted for ranking. Candidates who obtain such minimum qualifying marks as fixed by the Commission are summoned for an interview for a Personality Test. The number of candidates called for interview are generally twice the number of vacancies to be filled in. The interview carries 250 marks with no minimum qualifying marks.

Marks obtained by the candidates in the Main Examination (written part as well as interview) determines their final ranking. Candidates are allocated to various services on the basis of their ranks in the examination and the preferences expressed by them for different services.

Although passing the examination is the primary route to enter the I.A.S., there are two other ways in which members can be recruited into the service. The first is the emergency or special recruitment while the second alternative route is by promotion from the state civil services.

After the final selection the candidates are imparted training at the Lal Bahadur Shastri National Academy of Administration at Mussoorie. There is difference in training progremme of I.A.S. and other services, common emphasis being laid on imparting training to equip officers for undertaking programmes of socio-economic development. The training period for an entrant to the I.A.S. both at Mussoorie and in the district spans about twenty-eight months before he is placed in an independent position.[25]

There is no central cadre of the I.A.S. and the new recruits confirmed in the service are permanently placed by the central government in a particular state cadre. The I.A.S. officers come on deputation to the centre. However, the I.A.S. officers are governed by the rules framed by the central government.[26]

Thus, we find that there is a continuity of British administrative tradition in the new setting after independence. The India Administrative Service constituted on the model of I.C.S. has maintained its elitist character.[27] Even the recent changes introduced by the U.P.S.C. in the system of recruitment maintain the generalist liberal orientation of the recruits.

New Tasks

After independence, the total environment and ethos of the country underwent a qualitative change and the bureau-

25. Singhi, *op. cit.*, p. 42.
26. *Ibid.*
27. Bhambhri "Administrators in a Changing Society", *op. cit.*, p. 24.

cracy which has its genesis in the colonial period has now to function in a new context, a context which is fundamentally different from that of the British regime. The first is the changed political context. Democratic elections, political parties, competitive politics, and parliamentary government provided a radically new dimension. The bureaucrats have now to function in a representative and democratic set-up where he is not only responsible to the higher ups in his cadre but also to the elected representatives of the peoples. The democratic institutions like the cabinets, legislatures, political parties and pressure groups provide the framework of purposes, goals and resources within which the bureaucracy has now to operate. "It has to be sensitive to the policies laid down by the Cabinets and Legislatures, the values and purposes of the leadership, and the interests and pressures of political parties and socio-economic groups".[28] Secondly, the ideal of welfare state has been accepted under the Constitution. The government has also emphasized its commitment to the goal of socialism. The goals of nation-building and modernisation have been given first priority by the planners and policy-makers. The execution of all these programmes and activities are dependent upon the effective functioning of administrative machinery. Thirdly, the administrators are no more the rulers. They are the servants of the people. They are required to give up their authoritarian attitude and be dedicated to the service of the people. They are not to serve the people from above. To develop a society which is largely backward and traditional, the administrators have to go to the villages not only to collect revenue and taxes but also to educate the people, to help them in improving agricultural yields, to conduct election, to build roads and bridges and to help the sick and ailing persons. In other words, they have now to carry on administration with participation and co-operation of the people. Emphasising the new context, role and responsibilities of the administrators in independent India, late Shri G.B. Pant pointed out :

28. C.N. Bhalerao, "Bureaucracy as an Institution of Modernisation : Some Issues", *Administrative Change in India* (ed.) Ramesh K. Aurora (Jaipur : Aalekh Publishers, n. d.), p. 62.

> "To serve the villagers, you have to identify yourself with rural life ; to find joy in the air you breaths and consciousness [*sic*] of the fact that you are engaged in the act of building of a new society. You have to train people in the art of life and in the art of living. You have to see that they move, they move onward and they are not pushed onward artificially. Let them learn the art which will enable them to secure for themselves what you want them to possess. Unless you try to influence without imposing something from above, your success will be short-lived".[29]

Finally, with the establishment of democracy after independence, the Indian masses began to be politicised and conscious of their own rights. As a result of government initiative and programmes, the social structure and values also gradually began to undergo changes. The universal adult franchise and agro-industrial development has changed the basic Indian Philosophy, a philosophy under which the people were expected only to obey the government.[30] The concept of 'Ma-baap Sarkar' is no more in existence. The bureaucracy has now come to function among the people who are conscious of their right and who not only obey but also make demands upon the administration. The new administrative system of India emphasizes "a public not parasitic in its relationship to the administrative system, but participant, a public which accepted duties as well as made demands, a public confident in administrative hierarchy and motivated to share in the responsibilities of development".[31]

Thus, under the new set-up, the area of bureaucratic functioning has enlarged both quantitatively and qualitatively. Its function is no longer limited to the maintenance of law and order ; it has now to undertake vast and complex tasks

29. Quoted by Mathur, *op. cit.*, p. 6.
30. Bhambhri, "Administrators in a Changing Society", *op. cit.*, p. 19.
31. S.J. Eldersveld, V. Jagannadham and A.P. Barnabas, *op. cit.*, pp. 7-8.

of nation-building and socio-economic development. But what role does the bureaucracy actually play in this task of nation-building and socio-economic development ? If newspaper accounts, the criticisms voiced in the Parliament, State Legislatures and the public, the findings of research scholars and the criticisms of the Administrative Reforms Commission and similar Commissions in the States are any indication of bureaucratic performance, a gloomy picture appears as an answer to this question. Almost everyday, there are criticisms that the bureaucracy has failed in its task of nation-building and development. Not only has the Indian bureaucracy failed as an instrument of social change, it is also resistant to change within itself. Over the years, there has been an increase in corruption and inefficiency in the bureaucracy ; its independence, integrity and devotion to public interest have also been undermined. It is now widely recognised that such a bureaucracy is ill-equipped for the massive and complex tasks of nation-building and socio-economic development.

But why has the bureaucracy failed in its task of nation-building and socio-economic development ? In the present study, we propose to examine this question with particular reference to the higher bureaucracy in Meghalaya. The reason for restricting the scope of our enquiry to the higher achelon of bureaucracy is that, being the managerial-group in the bureaucracy, it is more likely to have a direct bearing on economic, political and other kinds of national development. It is the higher bureaucrate who are called upon to provide policy counsel, to assist in the formulation of programmes, and to engage in the management and direction of administration for translating policy-goals into realities.

The hypothesis, which is the subject of the present enquiry, is that the bureaucracy is unable to perform its role effectively in the task of nation-building and development because of the divergence between its structural-behavioural elements and the new demands placed upon it. With its old and worn-out structure, the bureaucracy is called upon to provide leadership in the stupendous task of nation-building and development.

This divergence is one of the most important sources of strain upon the bureaucracy and leads to a number of problems which need critical examination.

Guided by the above hypothesis, an attempt is made in this study to identify some of the problems the higher bureaucracy faces in Meghalaya in the performance of its role as an instrument of development. The present study has been divided into seven chapters. Chapter one gives an outline of the present study while chapter two describes the setting and sample of the study. Chapter three deals with the socio-economic background of the bureaucrats, and chapter four, with the structural framework in which they work. In chapter five, we deal with the strains resulting from democratisatisation and in chapter six, we analyse bureaucratic dysfunctions. Finally, chapter seven sums up the study dovetailing the preceeding discussion along with a study of the value commitment of the bureaucrats.

2

Setting and Sample

The purpose of this chapter is to describe the setting of this study and the place of the respondents in their social and work context. It has now been realised that the bureaucratic organisation cannot function in a vacuum but in close interaction with the environment of which it is a part. Thus, to understand the functioning of bureaucracy, it is necessary to understand the socio-economic context in which it functions. And, since, the present study refers to the problems of higher bureaucracy in Meghalaya, it will be pertinent to discuss here the socio-economic conditions of the state in which our respondents function.

Meghalaya came into being by carving out the two hill districts of the former Assam state, namely, the Khasi and Jaintia Hills district and the Garo Hills district on April 2, 1970, as an autonomous state and became a full-fledged state on January 21, 1972. The state is located in the eastern part of India and lies between 25°5″ and 26°10″ north latitude and between 98°47″ and 97°47″ east longitude and now consists of five districts: the Jaintia Hills district, the East Khasi Hills district, the West Khasi Hills district, the East

Garo Hills district and the West Garo Hills district. It is surrounded by six districts of Assam on three sides except in the south, on which side it has common boundary with Bangladesh. It is surrounded on the north by Goalpara, Kumrup and Nowgong districts of Assam, on the west by Goalpara district of Assam and part of Bangladesh, on the south by Cachar district of Assam and Bangladesh and on the east by Mikir Hills and North-Cachar Hills district of Assam. The state has its opening through Assam to the rest of India which is further connected with other parts of the country by a narrow corridor which runs for about fifty kilometres below the foot-hills of Bhutan and Sikkim.

The state covers a land surface of approximately 22,500 sq.kms. consisting mostly of mountainous terrains. According to the census of 1971, the state has a total population of 10,11,699 of which 5,20,967 are male and 4,90,732 are female. Thus, the number of females per 1,000 males stands to be 942 according to 1971 census. The percentage of tribals in the state's population is 80.48 percent and that of Scheduled Castes is 0.38 percent. The rest 19.14 percent are of mixed nature consisting of Assamese, Bengalis, Nepalese, Biharis, Marwaris, etc.[1] The growth of population has been at the rate of 2.70 percent per annum during the decade 1961-71. The density of population per square kilometre according to 1971 census is 45, having risen from 33 in 1961.

The population of the state is predominantly rural. There are six towns in the state with a population of 1,47,170 which constitute approximately 14.50 percent of the state's population according to 1971 census. The rural population consists of about 8,64,529 and account for 85.64 percent of the state's population (1971 census). The number of inhabited villages in the state is 4,583, the average population per village being 186 persons.

1. *Statistical Hand Book*, Meghalaya, (Shillong : Directorate of Economics, Statistics and Evaluation, Government of Meghalaya, 1978), p. 10.

Socially, there prevails a matrilineal sysem in the state. Mother is the head of the family and the youngest daughter is the heir of parents. From the point of view of religion, Christianity is the religion of the greater number of population in the state (46.98%) followed by other religions and persuasions (31.45%) : Hinduism (18.50%), Islam (2.60%), Buddhism (0.19%), Jainism (0.12%) and Sikhism (0.03%).[2] Linguistically, it is of mixed type with English as the state language. The percentage of literacy in the state as per 1971 census is 29.49 against the all-India average of 29.45 percent.

Economically, the state is very backward. There is no big and medium industry in the state. The only industry worth mentioning, viz., the Cherrapunjee Cement Factory, has a total capital investment of approximately Rs. 5 crores. The worker's percentage ratio in Meghalaya is 44.92 according to 1971 census. More than 80 percent of the workers are traditionally engaged in agriculture either as cultivators or agricultural labourers. Most of the cultivators are small and marginal farmers.[3] The employment opportunity outside the agricultural sector is low due to the backward economic conditions of the state and the lack of industrialisation.

Again, the traditional prevailing pattern of agriculture by jhumming or shifting cultivation in large areas of the state acts as a limiting factor in the growth of the economy in the rural areas. According to a recent rough estimate, about 75,000 hectares of land are annually put under this method of shifting cultivation[4] and about 42 percent of the tribal population of the state (approximately 3.50 lakhs) is dependent upon shifting cultivation or jhumming.[5]

2. *Statistical Hand Book,* Meghalaya, *op. cit.*, p. 8.

3. *Draft Annual Plan,* 1978-79, (Planning Department, Government of Meghalaya), p. i.

4. D.T. Zimba, *Geography of Meghalaya,* (Shillong : Lama Villa, n.d.), p. 57.

5. *Draft Annual Plan,* 1978-79, *op. cit.*

Communication and transport system, one of the most important prerequisites of economic development, is very much lacking in Meghalaya. Being a hilly state, there is no rail-road or water transport in the state. The principal means of communication in the state is roadways which is again not sufficiently developed. There are a few all weather roads which are also not sufficient. At present, Meghalaya contains 15 kilometres of road per 100 square kilometres compared to the all-India average of 29 kilometres.[6]

Another problem of the state is the development of border areas. This border area comprises about 4,960 square kilometres with a population of approximately 2.30 lakhs according to the 1971 census. Thus, about 22 percent of the total area and 23 percent of the state's rural population are under these areas which, prior to the partition of the country, were totally dependent upon trade with those markets which are now within the jurisdiction of Bangladesh. As a result, the economy of these areas has been ruined with the partition and inspite of the efforts made before the state of Meghalaya came into being, the economy of these areas could not be rehabilitated.[7]

While the entire state is backward on the basis of economic indicators, there are areas which are considered to be especially backward in the state. Again, there are most backward pockets within those especially backward areas.

In order to deal with the problem of socio-economic backwardness of the state, the government launched in April, 1978, the new medium term plan of five years from 1978-79 to 1982-83. In the planning process the methodology of rolling plan was introduced which means that formulating the five year plan for the period 1978-83 during the year 1978-79, and after taking note of development till then, the plan for 1983-84 would be projected. A similar process would continue and in

6. *ibid.*
7. *Ibid.*

due time there would be a five year plan.[8]

The priority sectors in the Draft Proposal of the Annual Plan for the year 1978-79 were agriculture, development of communication, provision of drinking water in the rural areas, extension of educational benefits particularly in the rural areas, integrated development of border areas and development of small industries based on the utilisation of mineral and agro-forest resources of the state.[9]

The success of such an ambitious plan depends upon the implementing machinery i.e. the administration, for a proper understanding of which it is necessary to know the traditional political institutions and administration in the area which now comprises Meghalaya.

Originally, Meghalaya (the Garo Hills district and the United Khasi and Jaintia Hills district) was administered by the traditional chiefs with the help of their associates. In the Garo Hills, Nokmaship was the traditional system of administration. But after the British annexation, the office of Laskar was introduced in Garo Hills by David Scott in the year 1824.[10] A Laskar was generally a chief over a group of villages and Nokma was the head of the village subordinate to Laskar.[11] Laskar among the Garos performed the function of both rural police and an honorary magistrate. Minor cases could be heard and settled by the Laskar although appeal could be made to the District Magistrate against the decision of the

8. S.D. Kongwir, Deputy Chief Minister, Meghalaya, *Review of the Implementation of Development Schemes and Programmes for 1978-79 : A supplement to the Budget Speech 1978-79*, (Government of Meghalaya), p. 1.

9. *Draft Annual Plan*, 1978-79, *op. cit.*, p. iii.

10. V. Venkata Rao, *A Century of Tribal Politics in North-East India 1874-1974*, (First ed., Delhi : S. Chand and Co. Ltd., 1976), p. 106.

11. Edward T. Dalton, *Tribal History of North-East India*, (Delhi : Cosmo Publications, 1973), p. 64.

Laskar.[12] However, in 1865, Zimmadari system was introduced in the Garo Hills which was only an extension of the Laskar system.[13]

The Khasi Hills, at the time of British annexation in 1833, was found to be divided into several states under hereditary chiefs forming a Confederacy.[14] After the British annexation, the Siem or the chiefs administered the Khasi Hills in subsidiary alliance with the British Crown. The Siem or the chiefs assisted by Darbar (Assembly) conducted the administration under the over-all control and supervision of the Deputy Commissioner of the United Khasi and Jaintia Hills district.[15] Petty cases could be heard by the Siems. Only heinous offences or the cases in which subjects of the different states were concerned, were tried by the court of Political Agent, and later on, by that of the Deputy Commissioner.[16]

Before the British annexation, the Jaintia Hills was ruled by the Raja who had diplomatic relations with Ahom and Kachari Kings of Assam.[17] Raja was assisted in the administration of the state by Dolois and Sirdar who belonged to special castes and were elected. The Dolois, in turn, had subordinate officers called Pators, Basans and Dans to assist him in his functioning.[18] The British annexed the Jaintia Hills in 1835, and retained the old system of Doloiship and Sirdarship. The Dolois were empowered to hear all Civil cases and Criminal complaints not of a serious nature.[19]

12. S. Barkataki, *Tribes of Assam,* (New-Delhi : National Book Trust of India, 1969), pp.25-26.
13. Venkata Rao, *op.cit.*, p.107.
14. Dalton, *op.cit.*, p.55.
15. Venkata Rao, *op.cit.*, pp.116-117.
16. Barkataki, *op.cit.*, p.32.
17. *Ibid.*, p.42.
18. *Ibid.*, p.45.
19. *Ibid.*, p.46.

It is clear from the preceding discussion that the Britishers did not disturb the traditional administrative system much and allowed the traditional system to function under the suzerainty of the British Empire in India. This was probably because of the fact that it was not possible for the British administrators to comprehend the traditional system of rites and practices and above all, the hilly region was not considered to be beneficial to the British Empire.

Thus, there was a difference in the administration of the Plains and the Hills. In the hill areas there was minimum interference with the powers and functions of the chiefs. However, in 1872-73, it was found to be an urgent necessity to regulate the commercial relations of British subjects with the frontier tribes and accordingly a Regulation framed by the Lt. Governor of Bengal, subsequently approved by the Governor-General-in-Council, empowered the Lt. Governor to prescribe a line to be called Inner Line in each tribal area beyond which no British subject and certain classes of foreign residents could pass without a licence or a pass.[20]

The Montague-Chelmsford Report recommended in 1917 that the typically backward tracts should be excluded from the jurisdiction of the Reformed Council, and no legislation should be enacted in the Legislative Council affecting the areas. Legislation for such areas should be made entirely by means of Regulation made by the Governor-General-in-Council.[21]

The Government of India Act, 1919, empowered the Governor-General-in-Council to declare any territory in British India to be a backward area. Following this provision, the Governor-General-in-Council declared the Garo Hills and the British portion of the Khasi and Jaintia Hills, other than Shillong Municipality and the Cantonment area, as backward

20. Venkata Rao, *op.cit.*, pp.45-46.

21. *Ibid.*, p.47.

tracts on 3rd January, 1921. It also declared that all laws, provincial or Indian, solely intended for these tracts be applied only as directed by the Governor-General-in-Council and with such modifications as might be made by him. The Governor was, further, authorised to apply provincial laws to these areas with or without modifications.[22]

Following the recommendations of the Simon Commission, the White Paper of 1933 proposed the classification of hilly areas of Assam into two : Excluded and Partially Excluded Areas, and this proposal was contained in the Government of India Bill, 1935.[23] Under the Government of India Act, 1935, tribal areas were classified into three : Excluded, Partially Excluded and Frontier Areas, and the Garo Hills and the British portion of Khasi and Jaintia Hill districts were brought under the Partially Excluded Areas.[24] The administration of Partially Excluded Areas was brought under the Provincial Government although the Governor was given the discretionary power to modify or withhold the application of any law passed by the Provincial Legislature.

Before independence, when the political future of India was being discussed, the question of the administration of tribal areas came up before different committees and subcommittees. Following the suggestion of the Cabinet Mission, the Constituent Assembly appointed a sub-committees called the North-East Frontier (Assam) Tribal and Excluded Areas Committee with Gopinath Bardoloi as its Chairman (commonly the committee came to be known as Bardoloi Committee).[25] The Bardoloi Committee, being influenced by the ideas of social anthropoligists of non-assimilation, recommended the establishment of both autonomous and non-autonomous District Council for looking after the administration of tribal

22. *Ibid.*, p. 52.
23. *Ibid.*, pp. 55-81.
24. *Ibid.*, p. 153.
25. *Ibid.*, p. 157.

affairs.[26] Despite vehement opposition by some members, the recommendation of the Bardoloi Committee was accepted by the Constituent Assembly on the ground that the tribes of North-East India has a separate culture distinct from the tribes of the rest of India, the preservation of which required separate administrative arrangements.[27] Accordingly, in 1952, the Khasi and Jaintia Hills District Council and the Garo Hills District Council came into being. Later on, in 1964, the Jaintia Hills was separated from the Khasi Hills and constituted into a District with a District Council of its own.[28]

Thus, at present there are three District Councils in Meghalaya : the Khasi Hills District Council, the Jaintia Hills District Council and the Garo Hills District Council. The District Councils deal with the allocation, occupation or use of both agricultural and non-agricultural land other than reserved forests and are responsible for the management of forests other than reserved forests ; the use of canal or water courses for the purposes of agriculture and to control, prohibit or permit jhumming or other forms of shifting cultivation. The District Council has also the power to make laws regarding the appointment of chiefs or headmen, their succession, inheritance of property, marriage and other social customs. Further, the District Council has the power to establish or manage primary schools, dispensaries, markets, cattle-pounds, ferries, etc. For the execution of its laws, the District Councils has a Executive Committee with the Chief Executive Member (C.E.M.) at the head and two other members. The Chief Executive Member is elected by the District Council and the other members of the Committee are appointed by the Governor on the recommendation of the Chief Executive Member.

The District Council has its own court for hearing minor

26. *Ibid.*, pp. 176-182.

27. *Ibid.*, pp. 182-186.

28. *Ibid.*, p. 199.

cases, though appeals can be made against its decision. The District Council has its own administrative staff for the management of its affairs.

Though on paper it appears that the District Council is an autonomous body, in practice, its autonomy is considerably eroded. The District Council is virtually a body subordinate to the State Government because it has to function under the supervision of the Governor who acts generally in accordance with the advice of the Council of Ministers, though he has discretionary powers in this regard. The Governor is authorised to suspend or dissolve or supersede a District Council. Further, the creation of the State of Meghalaya dealt a serious blow to the power and prestige of the District Council. Before the creation of the state, tribal sentiments found expression through the platform of the District Councils, which can now be expressed from a more important platform, the platform of the State Cabinet and the State Legislative Assembly.

However, the administration in Meghalaya is carried on by both the District Council and the State Government. The District Council looks after matters which are more traditional and customary in nature and the rest are managed by the State Government. In other words, a major burden of administration falls upon the State Government except the administration which is of customary nature.

For carrying on the administration of the state, the Meghalaya Government had a total of 16,556 employees in the year ending 1975, of which 14,577 were male and 1,979 were female.[29] Out of these 16,556 employees, 789 are gazetted, 10,644 are non-gazetted and 5,123 are Grade IV employees.[30] A caste and tribe-wise break-up of the employees shows that Scheduled Tribe is the most dominant group which accounts for 58.39 percent (Hills Tribe, 56.41 percent

29. *Statistical Hand Book*, Meghalaya, *op. cit.*, p. 90.

30. *Ibid.*, p. 91.

and Plains Tribe, 1.98 percent) of the total employees followed by others (i.e. the general category which constitutes 22.79 percent), other backward classes (14.08 percent) and Scheduled Castes (4.74 percent).[31] (For distribution of State Government employees according to Caster/Tribes and status as on 31st March, 1975, see table 2 : 1).

Against this universe of 16,556 employees, the sample of the present study enlists only 110 employees. Since this study deals with the higher bureaucracy in Meghalaya, all the respondents in this sample are gazetted class I employees of the State Government. This sample of 110 bureaucrats constitutes about 13.94 percent of a total of 789 gazetted employees of the State Governments. Originally, this sample had 130 bureaucrats. But 20 of them either did not return the questionnaire or could not be contacted. Numerical strength of the employees in the sample, according to their service, stands as follows :

Indian Administrative Service	...	25
Assam Civil Service	...	15
Meghalaya Civil Service	...	40
Meghalaya Health Service	...	10
Meghalaya Engineering Service	...	20
TOTAL =	...	110

The respondents in this sample belong to all the major departments—those of Home, Industry, Agriculture, Health, Education, Social Welfare, Community Development, Construction, Engineering, Border Areas Development, Forests, Road Transport Communication, etc. Vertically, the sample includes low, middle and high position bureaucrats. Horizontally, both the Headquarters and Field Officers are included in the sample—from the Secretary to the Community Development Department down to the B.D.O., from the Secretary to the Home Department down to the Extra-Assistant Commissioner in the District, and from the Secretary to the Department of Health down to the Medical Officer.

31. *Ibid.*, p. 92.

3

Socio-Economic Background

Now the pertinent question is : who are the bureaucrats ? To find an answer to this, study of the socio-economic background of the bureaucrats is imperative. This study of socio-economic background of the bureaucrats is of special significance in a stratified society like India where the forces of caste and Kinship Influence the social life and where acute disparities exist in the standard of living and sub-culture among various groups and regions. The existence of inequality between the elite and the general masses and the slow process of occupational mobility emphasize the need for a study of the socio-economic background of the bureaucrats.[1]

In fact the study of socio-economic background of the bureaucrats gives rise to an important question: How far is the higher bureaucracy representative of society ? This representative character of bureaucracy is of great importance to a democratic country because it helps in the articulation of values and interests of different classes and strata which are brought to bear upon the decisions taken and policies formu-

1. Singhi, *op. cit.*, p. 55.

lated by it.[2] Norton E. Long goes so far as to say that representative bureaucracy is a better sample of the masses than the democratic legislature. He points out that important interests, which are malrepresented or unrepresented in the legislature, receive effective representation through administrative channels. It can save democratic process from being bogged down and can come to be recognised as the "great fourth branch of government".[3] It is more so in a society like India which is divided into castes, religious groups and linguistic and regional sub-divisions. The divisions of castes being based on the accident of birth are more rigid than class divisions because the former are ascriptive. One's status in them cannot be achieved, and consequently, there is less social mobility. This division of society makes it desirable that the country's bureaucracy should represent different castes and religious groups and also the different regions, so that, all the sections of the society with diverse interests can find representation in the formulation and implementation of policies. In the absence of this, there is the probability of sectional or parochial sympathies and even loyalties of the bureaucrats influencing their work leading to a neglect of the interests of the unrepresented sections. As Kelsall has shown, the middle-class origin of the British Civil Service is a factor responsible for its being out of touch with the problems of the working class.[4]

The class origin of the bureaucrats has an important bearing upon the functioning of bureaucracy, because it is generally recognised that an administrator brings with him certain attitudes and values which he develops before joining

2. V. Subramaniam, *Social Background of India's Administrators*, (Publication Division, Ministry of Information and Broadcasting, Government of India, New Delhi, 1971), p. 3.

3. Norton E. Long, "Bureaucracy and Constitutionalism", *The American Political Science Review*, Vol. XLVI, No. 3 (September 1952), pp. 808-818.

4. Subramaniam, *op. cit.*, p. 4.

the administration, and the development of these attitudes and values is influenced by the familial, social and other environmental conditions in which the administrator is brought up. The attitudes and values which the bureaucrats develop before joining the bureaucracy greatly influence his future course of action. As Strauss points out, "the administrator is not a self-contained and self-regulating mechanism, but an instrument for the furtherance of specific social interests, and, therefore, intimately concerned with the world at large and its problems".[5] Although it is a fact that the bureaucratic cultural pattern in which he works may either modify or reinforce his attitudes and values, this does not diminish the importance of the attitudes and values that he develops prior to joining the bureaucracy.[6]

Related to the representativeness of the higher bureaucracy, a question may be raised here as to how far does the background of the bureaucrats reveal the regional, linguistic, social and cultural heterogenity. The answer to this question may help us in understanding the contribution of higher bureaucracy to the preservation of the unity of the nation[7] as well as to the developmental process. As H. Rai and S.P. Singh say in regard to the latter : "it has to be considered whether the bureaucracy, with its present social background, can enthusiastically support and sincerely carry out the government policy aimed at a large-scale radicalization of the socio-economic structures of the country".[8]

5. Quoted by Bansal, *op. cit.*, pp. 99-100.

6. Ramashray Roy, *The Bureaucracy and Development : The Case Study of Indian Agriculture*, (First ed., New Delhi : Manas, 1975), p. 17.

7. Singhi, *op. cit.*, p. 57.

8. Haridwar Rai and Sakendra Prasad Singh, "Indian Bureaucracy : A Case for Representativeness", *The Indian Journal of Public Administration*, Vol. XIX, No. 1 (January-March, 1973), p. 1.

In the remaining section of this chapter, an attempt is made to study the age-group, sex, place of birth, provincial background, religion, nature of schooling and educational qualifications, of the bureaucrats and their fathers' education, occupation and income.

Age Group

Age of the bureaucrats is an important factor in their functioning and value orientations. At a young age, one is considered to be more hard-working, energetic and full of initiative and the spirit of enterprise than in one's old age. Later years of one's career are marked by maturity, thoughtfulness and a cautious approach. Man acquires experience with his age which helps him in taking decisions and formulating policies in the light of his past experience. And the experience which one gains with one's age also shapes and reshapes one's values which have an impact upon oneself and the organisation or unit of the system of which one is a part.

The principle of early age recruitment advocated by Lord Macaulay has been a feature of Civil Service recruitment in India since the days of the East India Company. At present the minimum age limit for competitive examinations in State and all-India services is twenty-one years and the maximum age limit is twenty-eight years[9] in the case of Central and all-India services. The maximum age limit in case of State services vary from State to State. In the case of Meghalaya, the maximum age limit is 27 years.[10]

9. Till 1978, the minimum age limit for I.P.S. was 20 years and the maximum age for all-India and Central services was 26 years including I.P.S. But following the Kothari Commission Report, the U.P.S.C. now conducts a combined Civil Service Examination for which the minimum age limit is 21 years and the maximum age limit is 28 years. The maximum age is relaxable by 3 to 8 years in different cases.

10. *Meghalaya Civil Service Rules, 1975*, (Shillong : The Government Press, 1975), p. 5.

In our present study of higher bureaucracy in Meghalaya, it is found that the higher bureaucracy is dominated by the middle-age group bureaucrats i.e. the age group of 31 to 40 and 41 to 50 years. 46.36 per cent of the bureaucrats in the sample belong to the age group of 31 to 40 years and 31.82 per cent belong to 41 to 50 years of age.[11] Only 16.36 per cent of the bureaucrats in the sample belong to the age group of 51 to 60, when in the age group of 21 to 30 there are only 5.46 per cent bureaucrats. This poor representation of the younger age-group in the higher bureaucracy is due to the fact that after 1975, no recruitment was made to the Meghalaya Civil Service till now.

Again, if we classify the position occupied by the bureaucrats according to their service, we find that bureaucrats belonging to the I.A.S. occupy the upper and middle positions of the hierarchy. The I.A.S. officers who are even below 40 years of age, sometimes occupy the uppermost rung of the hierarchy, whereas very few of their contemporaries in the State services occupy the middle positions, most of them being in the lower ranks of the hierarchy.

On the other hand, there are some variations with regard to the officers belonging to technical services. Technical officers occupy upper positions at an early age. This is probably because of the fact that Meghalaya is a newly created state where there are new developmental activities and these developmental activities require a large number of technical experts and consequently, there are ample opportunities for them to occupy higher positions at an early age.

Sex

Sex is an important factor in the study of bureaucracy in India where the position of women is comparatively low. There is also a popular assumption that women are

11. See Tabl• 3 : 1.

both physically and intellectually weak in comparison with men and the proper sphere of women is the management of household affairs. At the beginning of this century, there were very few women who were in public service. But with the passage of time, this barrier has been broken and especially after independence more and more women has been competing for and joining the public service. At present, an increasing number of women candidates are joining the all-India and Central Services.

Meghalaya being a matrilineal society, the question of the lower position of women does not arise here. Women occupy a respected and honourable position in the society, and, therefore, it is of special interest to study the sex of higher bureaucrats in a matrilineal state.

In our sample, there is one woman in the I.A.S., one in the A.C.S. and seven in the M.C.S.[12] The small number of females in the I.A.S. can be explained by the fact that the females prefer the Indian Administrative Service less because it is an all-India Service subject to posting in any part of India which unsettles them. This also accounts for the small representation of women in the State services. Despite the matrilineal nature of society, women do not prefer Administrative Services as they involve work in any part of the state.

Provincial Background

Provincial background of the bureaucrats is an important dimension in the study of bureaucracy in a country like India where great diversities exist within the states. This sometimes give rise to communalism, casteism and sub-regionalism. The new State of Meghalaya which was carved out of Assam as a result of the process of "Assamization" has given more overt expression to the feeling of regionalism. This feeling of regionalism got a new philip during the last general election to Meghalaya Legislative Assembly in February, 1978. Almost all political parties in their election manifestoes devoted a

12. See Table 3 : 2.

substantial space to the pledge of preserving tribal culture and heritage against the influx of outsiders from other parts of India and for the reservation of seats in government jobs for the tribals.[13] The local sentiment or the sentiment of regionalism has struck its roots so deep that some political leaders opposed the installation of some industries and the setting up of Railway tracks in some parts of Meghalaya on the ground that these will invite the influx of more outsiders in the State.[14] There is a fear in the mind of the local people that if people from outside the state are allowed to come and settle in Meghalaya, the demographic structure of the state will be adversely affected and a time will come when the so-called tribal culture and tribal identity would be lost. This fear is reflected in the purposed Inner Line Permit Bill [15] and the Land Transfer Act.[16] The feeling of regionalism manifested in its worst form in rioting and bloodshed when it capitalised by some political parties who started a movement for the deportation of outsiders in the name of foreign nationals. Even some Central Government employees belonging to a particulars community were served with notices for appearing before the Magistrate with appropriate documents to prove themselves as Indian citizens.

13. For details, see the *Election Manifestoes of APHLC, HSPDP and Congress Party* during the second general election to the Meghalaya Legislative Assembly.

14. See *Meghalaya Legislative Assembly Debates,* Vol. 1, No. 2 (Budget Session, 1973), p. 36, Vol I, No. 2, (March Session, 1974), p.13 and Vol X, No. 2 and (Budget Session, 1978) pp. 30-31.

15. The Inner Line Permit Bill sought to restrict the entry of outsiders in the state by introducing a system of permit which an outsider must obtain before entering into the state and could not stay longer than the time as permitted.

16. The Meghalaya Transfer of Land (Regulation) Act, 1971 (commonly called Land Transfer Act) seek to restrict the transfer of land from tribals to non-tribals and from non-tribals to non-tribals.

    Supporting the Meghalaya Transfer of Land (Regulation) Act, 1971, Shri Hoover Hynniewta said "we have been able to

In the Meghalaya State, forty percent of the Government jobs are received for the Khasis, forty percent for Garos, five percent for other Scheduled Castes and Scheduled Tribes and the remaining fifteen percent for general category. A person not belonging to any of the Scheduled Tribes of Meghalaya, is required to produce a Resident Certificate to the affect that he is a permanent resident of Meghalaya before joining any job under the State Government. This has created a feeling of insecurity and frustration among the non-tribal residents of Meghalaya, most of whose fore-fathers were originally from out side the state, who came here for jobs and settled permanently. It is reported that the only job the non-tribals can hope to get in Meghalaya is in the Central Government establishments. Hence, the peoples other than the tribals frequently complain about the irrational reservation policy of the Government.

The Meghalaya tribals, on the other hand, are also not satisfied with the present position because the Meghalaya Government, having small establishments, cannot absorb all the job-seekers in the government service. There is also no industry worthy of name in the state to provide employment

maintain our racial identity because to a great extent land is still under our control and possession but once our lands are taken away from us through the unfettered and indiscriminate purchases by non-tribals the Hill people in no time be reduced to an insignificant minority in their traditional homeland... I repeat... that if we allow non-tribals to purchase land indiscriminately then before the long the peoples of Khasi Hills and Garo Hills will be reduced to a minority in their homeland. As a case in point, I will refer to the case of the Tripuris who, before the attainment of Independence constituted the ovrwhelming majority in the native state of Tripura. The position now has been reversed after the influx of refugees from East Pakistan immediately in the wake of Independence, so much, so that the Tripuris are having only 19 seats reserved for them in a House of 60. It is too much for me too say... that we donot like this fact to overtake us. So,... our very survival is inextricably linked up with the preservation of our ownership over land". See *Meghalaya Legislative Assembly Debates*, Vol. 1, No. 2 (March/April Session, 1979), pp. 34-35.

to the tribal youth coming out of schools, colleges and universities. Recently, a feeling has arisen which has been partly injected by the political parties in the minds of the tribal youth that it is only because of the non-tribal population that they are out of employment. This has led to a feeling of hatred and jealousy between the tribal and non-tribal population of the state, especially among the youth.

In the persent study, we find that 33.64 percent of the bureaucrats in our sample in Meghalaya are from outside the state and 66.36 percent of the bureaucrats are from within the state according to their place of birth.[17] But if we take into account the specialisation of the bureaucrats and their provincial background, it is found that the number of technical bureaucrats are greater from outside the state than the non-technical bureaucrats.[18] The percentage of outsiders in technical bureaucracy is 70.00 against the relevant percentage of 20.00 in non-technical bureaucracy. This dominant position of the outsiders in technical bureaucracy may be attributed to the non-availability of the facilities for technical education in Meghalaya. Students of Meghalaya aspiring for the study of medicine or engineering need to go to technical institutions in other states and consequently, the number of successful doctors and engineers are not proportionate to the needs of the state. Comparatively, there are sufficient facilities for general education in the state and 80.00 percent of the bureaucrats in the non-technical bureaucracy are from within the state.

Again, if we classify the provincial background of non-technical bureaucrats according to their service, we find that 44.00 percent of the bureaucrats belonging to the I.A.S. are from outside the state according to their place of birth. This percentage will be a little more if we take into account the place of residence of the bureaucrats at the time of their application. Although in case of the I.A.S. the 'withiners'

17. See Table 3 : 3.

18. See Table 3 : 4.

are a little more than the majority i.e. 56.00 percent ; in the case of the A.C.S. and M.C.S. they are overwhelmingly dominant. 80.00 percent of the bureaucrats belonging to the A.C.S. and 95.00 percent to the M.C.S. are from within the state. This difference of repesentation of the 'withiner' in the I.A.S. and State Services may be explained in terms of educational facilities available in the state. The Indian Administrative Service is by and large composed of the intellectually best endowed graduates. A tough competition for entry into the I.A.S. needs a high level of intellectual ability which can be developed if there are good facilities for higher education. But till 1974, post-graduate courses were beyond the reach of the general students in Meghalaya as there was no University in the state. It was only in 1973, that a Central University was established in Shillong and in 1975, an I.A.S. coaching centre also started functioning in that University. However, the over-representation of the 'withiner' in the State Services may be attributed to the limited nature of the competition both in terms of academic standard and the field of competition.

Rural-Urban Background

The underlying importance of the study of the rural-urban background of the bureaucrats is that it influences their norms, values and behaviour patterns which have an important bearing on their functioning. As the facilities available in urban areas are different from those of the rural areas, the process of socialisation also tends to be different in rural-urban settings. Persons living in urban areas are exposed to scientific and industrial development. Thus, the rural-urban background not only affects the functioning of bureaucracy but also the value-orientation of the bureaucrats which influences the strategy of development and modernisation.

In our sample, only 23.64 percent of the bureaucrats were born in rural areas while 76.37 percent were born in urban areas.[19] Thus, the rural-urban ratio in the higher bureaucracy is just the reverse of the rural-urban ratio in the state's population. This is the case if we take into account only the place of birth of the bureaucrats. But if we take into account the place where the bureaucrats lived until they entered the service instead of the place of birth, the urban influence would be far greater because of the movement from rural to urban areas for better educational facilities. Other studies also confirm this predominantly urban background of the higher bureaucrats. The study by Richard Taub in Bhubaneswar revealed a similar urban background of the higher bureaucrats.[20] The study by C.P. Bhambhri of the 273 I.A.S. recruits in two years (in 1966-67 and 1968-69) revealed that over 70.00 percent of the recruits had an urban background.[21] This high urban-centredness in recruitment reveals to a significant extent, the social limitations, in structural terms, on entry into the higher bureaucracy in India.

Among the non-technical bureaucrats, a very high percentage of the officers of the I.A.S. possess urban background (84.00 percent) followed by A.C.S. and M.C.S. 73.33 percent of the bureaucrats belonging to the A.C.S. and 65.00 percent of the bureaucrats belonging to the M.C.S. have had an urban background.

In the case of technical bureaucrats, doctors are found to be more urban in background than the engineers, 90.00 percent of the doctors and 85.00 percent of the engineers in the sample had urban background. Another feature to be noted here is that technical bureaucrats have more urban background than non-technical bureaucrats.[22] 86.67 percent of the technical bureaucrats and 72.50 percent of the non-technical

19. See Table 3 : 5.

20. Taub, *op. cit.*

21. Bhambhri, "Administrators in a Changing Society", *op. cit.*, p. 47.

22. See Table 3 : 6.

bureaucrats were found to have urban background. The more urban background of the technical bureaucrats is probably due to the specialised nature of study facilities which are not available in the rural areas.

Religious Background

India is committed to the ideals of secularism and equality of opportunity for Government employment irrespective of religion, caste or region. This has been well proved by electing persons from the minority community to the highest office under the Indian Constitution. Although religion is not a qualification for entering into public service, in order to be representative, public service must represent people of different religious communities as it helps in the articulation of values and interests of the different classes. Demands are not infrequent for the reservation of seats in the public services for those minority communities which are not well-represented. It will, therefore, be useful to examine whether different religious groups are represented in the higher bureaucracy of Meghalaya or not.

In the present study, it is found that Christianity is the religion of 60.00 percent of bureaucrats followed by Hinduism which is the religion of 36.36 percent of bureaucrats.[23] The Sikhs and Muslims are also represented and their percentage is 1.82 percent each. It is thus found that the Christians and Hindus are a little over-represented while the Buddhists, Jains and Traditionalists are not represented at all in our sample. The non-representation of the Buddhist and Jains may be interpreted in terms of the fact that Buddhist population in the state is mainly of the Tibetan Lamas and few traders while the Jains are mostly engaged in business. The over-representation of Hindus is due to their dominant position in technical bureaucracy (where they account for 60.00 percent of the bureaucrats while the Christians account for only 33.33 percent).[24]

23. See Table 3 : 7.
24. See Table 3 : 8.

Social Background

For the purpose of the present study, the caste groupings of Hindu society do not have much relevance as 60.00 percent of our respondents are Christians by religion, and in the tribal society of Meghalaya, there is no caste system. For studying the social composition of the bureaucracy in Meghalaya, it is useful to make a general classification : Scheduled Castes and Scheduled Tribes (SC and ST), on the one hand, and General, on the other, i.e. persons other than Scheduled Castes and Scheduled Tribes.

The Constitution of independent India has provided special safeguards to the Scheduled Castes and Scheduled Tribes in Government jobs and educational institutions in order to improve their lot. But this policy has given a new lease of life to caste divisions in India.[25] The policy of providing special benefits to persons on the basis of caste and tribe has caused dissatisfaction in the minds of the people and is responsible for creating social antagonism and tensions. The policy of special benefits was found to be one of the causes of increased atrocities on Harijans.[26] Recently, Bihar and Gujarat have witnessed violent agitations and destruction of properties over the question of reservation.[27]

In Meghalaya 85.00 percent of the jobs under State Government are reserved for Scheduled Castes and Scheduled Tribes (40.00 percent for the Khasis, 40.00 percent for Garos and 5.00 percent for other Scheduled Castes and Scheduled Tribes). Instead of this 85.00 percent reservation, it is found that 64.55 percent of the bureaucrats in our sample belong to Scheduled Tribes and 35.45 percent of the bureaucrats belong

25. M.N. Srinivas, *Caste in Modern India,* (Bombay : Asia Publishing House, 1977), p. 15.

26. *The Stateman* (Calcutta), October 3, 1978.

27. Editorial, *Anandabazar Patrika* (Calcutta), November 21, 1978.

to the general category.[28] The over-representation of the general category (the percentage of general category people other than Scheduled Castes and Scheduled Tribes in the state is slightly more than 19 percent) is due to their dominant position in the technical bureaucracy where they account for 63.33 percent.[29] In non-technical bureaucracy Scheduled Tribes bureaucrats account for 75.00 percent and general category bureaucrats, only 25.00 percent.

Fathers' Background : Educational Background

The bureaucrats' fathers' educational background is an important factor in understanding the socio-economic background of the bureaucrats. Education in ancient India was not professional and was the monopoly of Brahmins who were considered to be the symbol of learning. There was no modern system of mass education through schools and colleges. It was the Britishers who initiated modern education in India, and schools and colleges were gradually established. Although schools and colleges were established, their number was small and they were concentrated mostly in urban areas. Even after thirty-two years of our independence, educational facilities do not exist in every part of the country and till to-day about 70.00 percent of our people are illiterate. Higher education is very costly, and it is the monopoly of urban-living, middle-class elites. In Meghalaya the situation is further worse. Although the literacy rates is little higher than the all-India average of 29.45 percent, yet the facilities for higher education in the state are concentrated in the capital town of Shillong with some facilities available at a few district towns.

In this study, we find that 0.91 per cent of the fathers of bureaucrats are illiterate, 4.55 per cent are literate but without any formal education, 7.27 per cent have formal education

28. See Table 3 : 9.

29, See Table 3 : 10.

but are not matriculates, 10.91 per cent are matriculates, 20.91 per cent are under-graduates, 34.54 per cent are graduates and 16.36 per cent are post-graduates.[30] Thus, it shows that higher bureaucracy in a mass illiterate society reflects not only a literate but also a well-educated background which is in sharp contrast with the idea of representative bureaucracy. There exists a wide gap between the higher bureaucracy and the society in general. This study further confirms the fact that the career-pattern of the children depends upon the educational attainments of the parents. This sample shows that 24.00 per cent of the fathers of the I.A.S. are post-graduates ;[31] the relevant percentage in the case of the A.C.S. and the M.C.S. is 13.33 and 12.50 per cent, respectively.

Again, we find a difference between the educational background of the father and the specialisation of the bureaucrats.[32] The percentage of the fathers of technical bureaucrats is more in the educated category than their counterparts in the case of non-technical bureaucrats. This shows that educated parents prefer more the specialised and professional education for their children.

Occupation of the Fathers of Bureaucrats

Occupation is generally recognised as one of the indications of social status. Hence, in the study of bureaucracy in a developing society like India, occupation of the fathers of bureaucrats provides a convenient guide to the social origin of the bureaucrats themselves. Such a study also helps us to know, to what extent, the different strata of community provide the higher bureaucracy of the country and whether the major professional groups are represented in the country's bureau-

30. See Table 3 : 11.

31. In the category of post-graduate we have included all other degrees and diplomas which can be obtained only after graduation.

32. See Table 3 : 12.

cracy or not. Most of the studies[33] on higher bureaucracy suggest that the modern professional middle-class is over represented in it. But this is opposed to the principle representative bureaucracy in an equalitarian society.

In regard to the bureaucracy in Meghalaya, it is found that 11.82 per cent of the fathers of the bureaucrats have been engaged in agriculture, 10.00 per cent in business, 42.73 per cent in Government services, 13.64 per cent in professions like law, medicine, etc. and 14.54 per cent in teaching.[34] This is in great contrast with the socio-economic conditions in Meghalaya which is a rural state and where more than 80.00 per cent of the people are dependent upon agriculture.

Further, if we classify the occupation of the fathers and the specialisation of the bureaucrats, it is seen that fathers of technical bureaucrats are more in modern professions than the fathers of non-technical bureaucrats.[35] While 6.67 per cent of the fathers of technical bureaucrats have been engaged in agriculture, the relevant percentage for the fathers of non-technical bureaucrats is 13.75.

Fathers' Income

Related to fathers' occupation, fathers' income is another important dimension in the study of the socio-economic background of the bureaucrats. Income along with the occupation determines, to a great extent, the social status of a person and the resources available for the education of children. The career-choice of the child is largely dependent upon parental income. For getting a well-paid and prestigious job, one needs to be educated at a good college or university and the cost of good education is very high in India. It is

33. Bhambhri, "Administrators in a Changing Society", *op. cit.*, p. 93. Subramaniam, *op. cit.*, p. 93.

34. See Table 3 : 13.

35. See Table 3 : 14.

thus interesting to study the income group from which the higher bureaucrats come, as a representative bureaucracy must have in its fold members from different income groups of the society.

Though this survey has tried to find out the annual income of the fathers of the bureaucrats, it is very difficult to establish their annual income for the following reasons. Firstly, the difficulty arises because of the different sources of income, and secondly, there is a tendency on the part of the respondents either to over-estimate or to under-estimate the parental income. However, on the basis of the responses received from the respondents, the fathers' income of the bureaucrats have been divided into three groups : low, middle and high. Fathers with an annual income upto Rs. 5,000/- were grouped into low ; fathers with an annual income above Rs. 5,000/- but below Rs. 10,000/- were grouped into middle ; and father with an annual income Rs. 10,000/- were grouped into high category.

According to this scheme, we find that 43.62 per cent of the fathers of the bureaucrats belong to the middle income group while the percentage of low and high income groups are 30.91 and 17.27 per cent, respectively.[36] If we take into account the annual income of the fathers and specialisation of the bureaucrats, we find that technical bureaucrats come more from the higher income group than the non-technical bureaucrats.[37] This is probably because of the fact that specialised or technical education is more time-consuming and more costly, and consequently, less offered by the students of low income group family.

Educational Background of the Bureaucrats

Educational background of the bureaucrats is another important factor in understanding the socio-economic back-

36. See Table 3 : 15.

37. See Table 3 : 16.

ground of the bureaucrats. It is more so in a country like India where educational facilities are unevenly distributed. Here we shall study the nature of schooling and educational qualifications of the bureaucrats.

Nature of Schooling

The higher bureaucracy in India is, by and large, composed of the intellectually best endowed graduates. For entering into the higher bureaucracy, the candidates have to face a tough competition and need a high level of intellectual ability. The development of intellectual ability depends, to a great extent, upon the nature of education at the school and college level. "It is at the school stage that the foundation of the super-structure of the university education is laid down. For, what an individual learns in schools like what he learns at home from the members of his family, weighs heavily in determining which relatively full-time, functionally significant social roles he will be able to fulfil".[38]

But there is difficulty in classifying the schools. The common classification of public and private schools seems to be unsatisfactory because what is public in one context may be private in a different context. Of course, there is no fool-proof classification as every classification has some short-comings. However, we would classify the schools here on the basis of the medium of instruction i.e. English-medium schools and the vernacular schools.

Though the quality of education does not depend upon the medium through which knowledge is imparted, it is generally believed that some personal traits like smartness, discipline, fluent speaking, social graces, proficiency in sports and games, etc., are developed more in the English-medium schools than in the vernacular schools. And this is the reason

38. Prasad, *op. cit.*, p. 108.

why the well-to-do-families are eager to send their children in English-medium schools.

In the present sample, we find that 55.45 per cent of the bureaucrats have had English school background and 41.82 per cent of the bureaucrats have had vernacular school background.[39] Again, the non-technical bureaucrats are more from English school than from the technical bureaucrats. While 57.50 per cent of the non-technical bureaucrats have had English school background, the percentage of technical bureaucrats with English school background is only 50.00 per cent.[40]

This difference in schooling between the technical and non-technical bureaucrats can be explained by the fact that 70.00 per cent of the technical bureaucrats are from outside the state i.e., from other parts of India where there are good vernacular schools unlike Meghalaya. Secondly, for entry into the technical bureaucracy, candidates need not appear in an examination as in the case of non-technical bureaucracy. Since the introduction of competitive examinations for recruitment to the Indian Civil Services, English continued to be the medium of examination. It was in the recent past that U.P.S.C. has accepted the languages mentioned in the VIIIth schedule of the Constitution besides English as the media of examination for the I.A.S. and Allied Services examinations. In case of Meghalaya, English is the only medium of examinations for recruitment to Civil Services. And sometimes, English as the medium of examination acts as a disadvantage for candidates who are otherwise deserving. Suggesting regional languages as the media of competitive examinations, A. Avasthi observed, "I can say from personal experience that even the best boys in M.P. Universities fail to qualify in competitive examinations because their medium of instruction is Hindi. Thus a large portion of highly educated youth is

39. See Table 3 : 17.

40. See Table 3 : 18.

virtually barred from representation in these services because it [*sic*] does not [*sic*] know English adequately. There is close relationship between the English language, which till other day was the language of our rulers, anglicisation and snobbishness".[41] Thus, for entry into the non-technical bureaucracy, candidates with English school background have some edge over the candidates with the vernacular school background and this accounts for the fact that more non-technical bureaucrats have had English school background.

Educational Qualification

The study of educational qualifications also helps us in understanding the socio-economic background of the bureaucrats. The minimum educational qualifications prescribed for the I.A.S. and Allied Services and the State Services is the ordinary first degree of an university. But recent studies[42] suggest that the recruitment system for higher bureaucracy favours those candidates whose qualifications are higher than the minimum qualifications formally prescribed. In the present study, 47.27 per cent of the bureaucrats are post-graduates[43], 48.18 per cent are graduates and 2.73 per cent are under-graduates.[44] All the under-graduates belong to the Engineering Services who were promoted to their present positions. While the bulk of the post-graduates belong to the I.A.S., the least belong to the Engineering Services. Against 72.00 per cent post-graduates in the I.A.S., there are only 20.00 per cent post-graduates in the Engineering Services. The second largest number of post-graduates in the Health services i.e., 70.00 per cent, followed by the A.C.S. and the M.C.S. in

41. A. Avasthi, "The Challenge of Administrative Change in India", *Administrative Change in India,* ed., Arora, *op. cit.,* p. 22.

42. Taub, *op. cit.*, p. 72.

43. In the category of post-graduates, all other degrees and diplomas are included which can be obtained only after graduation.

44. See Table 3 : 19.

which the percentage of post-graduates are 46.67 and 40.00 per cent, respectively. The largest number of post-graduates in the I.A.S. confirms the fact that the I.A.S., like its predecessor the I.C.S., has in its fold highly qualified bureaucrats.

On the other hand, we find that post-graduates are more in non-technical bureaucracy than in technical bureaucracy. Against 51.25 per cent post-graduates in non-technical bureaucracy of this sample, there are only 36.67 per cent post-graduates in technical bureaucracy.[45] Thus, it appears that a simple graduation is enough for entering into the technical bureaucracy while it is not so in the case of non-technical bureaucracy. One of the possible reason for the fewer number of post-graduates in technical bureaucracy might be the longer time required for graduation in the technical field which makes the technical graduates fit for successfully competing for the examinations for entering into the public service. Another reason for this is the imbalance between demand and supply of the technically qualified personnel.

Summary

The socio-economic background of the bureaucrats reveals that the higher bureaucracy in Meghalaya, far from being representative in character, is a monopoly of the urban middle-class elites. After three decades of independence, there is very little change in the nature of higher bureaucracy. Still the rank of higher bureaucracy is virtually closed to men and women from the rural and other backward segments of society. Almost half of the bureaucrats in our sample have post-graduate degrees while more than half of the bureaucrats' fathers are either graduates or post-graduates. Our survey shows that higher bureaucrats come more from the modern professional middle-class families. Professions like Government services, teaching, law, medicine, etc. account for about seventy per cent of the bureaucrats' fathers' occupation with

45. See Table 3 : 20.

an annual income of Rs. 5,000/- and more. Only 11.82 per cent of the bureaucrats are found to have had agricultural background while 10 per cent have background of business. Along with the modern professional middle-class background, about 80.00 per cent of the bureaucrats come from urban areas. But this restricted nature of the higher bureaucracy in terms of its socio-economic background is in sharp contrast with the societal condition of Meghalaya in particular and India in general. This contrast between the socio-economic background of the higher bureaucrats and the societal condition is one of the problems the higher bureaucracy faces in Meghalaya because it raises the question of bureaucratic effectiveness in the implementation of development programmes which are essentially rural in character. This urban middle-class background underscores the ignorance of the higher bureaucrats about the conditions of the rural people and their problems. And without understanding the people, their conditions and problems, it is doubtful whether the bureaucrats can develop an empathy for them. Writing on the Civil Service of Pakistan, Goodnow observed, "The members of the CSP are far removed from the villagers who constitute the bulk of Pakistan's population. It is difficult for these civil servants to grasp the concept that the nation's future must be based on a substantial change in the character of the village and the outlook of its residents".[46]

46. Henry Frank Goodnow, *The Civil Service of Pakistan : Bureaucracy in a new nation*, (New Haven : Yale University Press, 1964), p. 239.

4

Organisation

After making a survey of the socio-economic background of the bureaucrats in Meghalaya, it is useful to study the organisation in which the bureaucrats work. An organisation exists in order to fulfil certain specific goals. Without specific goals, there can be no organisation ; and similarly, no goals for the common good can be achieved without organisations. That is why an organisation is defined as the co-ordinated activities of two or more persons for the achievement of some desired object. So, in an organisation there are two things: first, the co-ordinated effort, and second, the object. The second is dependent upon the first which, in turn, is dependent upon the willingness of the individual contributors. The willingness of the individual is not an independent variable to be assumed indefinitely. "The continuance of willingness also depends upon the satisfaction that are secured by individual contributors in the process of carrying out the purpose. If the satisfactions do not exceed the sacrifices required, willingness disappears, and the condition is one of organisational inefficiency. If the satisfactions exceed the sacrifices willingness persists, and the condition is one of efficiency of organisation.[1] And since the

1. Chaster I. Barnard, *The Functions of the Executive*, (Cam-

satisfaction is derived from both the structural willingness and functional aspects of an organisation, it is necessary to study these aspects of an organisation in which the bureaucrats work. Such a study will serve to highlight some of the problems the higher bureaucracy faces in Meghalaya as an instrument of development.

Organisation has two aspects : one is formal, and the other is informal. In this chapter, we shall first deal with formal aspect of the organisation, and then with the informal aspect followed by a study of the job-satisfaction of the bureaucrats.

Formal Organisation

By formal organisation is meant a formal structure of authority and a planned system of co-operative effort in which work sub-division are defined, arranged, and co-ordinated for the attainment of specific objectives. Though informal factors play a more important role in the functioning of an organisation, the formal organisation also influences the behaviour pattern of its members and deserves special attention. Pointing out the dangers of inadequate attention to formal organisation, Barnard wrote :

> To me, this failure of attention is like leaving a vital organ out of anatomy or its function out of physiology. Careful inspection of the observable actions of human beings in our society—their movements, their speech, and the thought and emotions evident from their action and speech—shows that many and sometimes most of them are determined or directed by their connection with formal organisations. This is most obviously true of the actions of persons as employees and housewives, which occupy perhaps one quarter of their time, but most persons in their 'non-working' hours are members or participants in other organisations.[2]

bridge : Massachusetts, Harvard University Press, 1951), p. 82.

2. *Ibid.*, pp. 3-4.

In this section, dealing with the formal bureaucratic organisation in Meghalaya, attention will be confined to the formal structure of bureaucracy in relation to hierarchy, procedures of work, and career pattern.

Hierarchy

Hierarchy is considered to be an universal principle of organisation and the Meghalayan bureaucracy is no exception. Like any other bureaucracy, the bureaucracy in Meghalaya is hierarchically organised, being linked by a chain from top to bottom in an unbroken manner. The Secretariat occupying a key position[3] in public bureaucratic system is located in the state capital, Shillong, with districts and blocks and villages as the main field units.

The working of the public bureaucracy can be broadly divided into two : general bureaucracy looking after the general administration and the technical bureaucracy looking after technical or specialised side of the administration. Corresponding to them, there are two types of departments : non-technical departments and technical departments. The non-technical departments deal with the affairs for which no specialised knowledge is required. The Secretariat in the capital and the office of the Deputy Commissioner in the district deal with the general affairs of the government. Technical departments are entrusted with work, the right performance of which requires specialised or technical skills in a definite field and persons recruited to such departments generally have technical qualifications acquired in technical institutions.[4]

Operating within a parliamentary framework of government, the State Chief Minister is both the political and

3. *Report of the Administrative Reforms Commission on Personnel Administration*, (Delhi : Government of India, August 1967), p. 37.
4. *Report of the Administrative Reforms Commission on Personnel Administration, op. cit.*, p. 38.

executive head who is assisted in his work by other Ministers. Each Minister is in-charge of one or more departments, depending upon the allocation of portfolios.[5] Although in theory, the Ministers are both the political and executive heads of their respective departments, in reality, the Ministers are more political heads than administrative heads. The administrative heads of the departments are the Secretaries who function under the direction of the Ministers.[6]

The bureaucracy of the state is headed by the Chief Secretary who is a senior member of the Indian Administrative Service. The Chief Secretary is responsible for the organisation and work in the government as a whole and operates directly under the control of the Chief Minister and the Cabinet.[7] The rest of the staff are organised ministry-wise under the administrative control of the Secretaries to Government (sometimes Commissioner or Special Secretary). The Secretaries are generally the members of the I.A.S., and sometimes a Secretary heads more than one department[8] and may be under the ministerial control of more than one minister, thus violating the principle of unity of command. Below the Secretary, there is a Joint-Secretary, who is also a member of the I.A.S. in Meghalaya. The Secretary or Joint-Secretary is assisted by Deputy-Secretaries who are drawn from both the I.A.S. and the State Services (A.C.S. and M.C.S.). Though the members of both the I.A.S. and State Services are appointed Deputy-Secretaries, it represents the beginning of career in case of the members of the I.A.S. while it is generally the end of the career in case of the members of the State Services. Below the Deputy Secretary, there are Under-Secretaries (also called Officers on Special Duty) who generally belong to the State Ser-

5. *Rules of Executive Business*, Cabinet Affairs and Personnel Departments, Government of Meghalaya, (Shillong : Assam Government Press, 1972), p. 98.
6. *Ibid.*
7. *Ibid.*, p. 107.
8. *Ibid.*, p. 98.

vices or are promoted from the rank of Superintendents. Below the Under-Secretary, there are the Superintendents of different branches who, in some cases, are assisted by Assistant Superintendents. Below the Superintendents and Assistant Superintendents, there are Upper Division Assistants and Lower Division Assistants who are entrusted with the different functions of the branch. Below the Upper Division Assistants, Stenographers and the Lower Division Assistants, there are Typists. At the bottom of the hierarchy, there are the Peons and menial workers (called class IV staff).[9]

At the district level, the Deputy Commissioner is the head of the administration, who is generally a member of the I.A.S. Besides his responsibility for the maintenance of law and order and the collection of revenue, the Deputy Commissioner is also responsible for different development projects in the district. The Deputy Commissioner is assisted in his work by Additional District Commissioners also known as Additional District Magistrates and a number of Extra-Assistant Commissioners. The Additional District Commissioners are the members of both the I.A.S. and the State Services while the Extra-Assistant Commissioners are drawn from the State Services.

The office of the Deputy Commissioner is the nerve centre of district administration and involves most complex and exacting responsibilities. Following the colonial tradition, many duties and responsibilities are assigned to the Deputy Commissioner which resulted in the diffusion of responsibility. In this connection, Dr. Paul H. Appleby has aptly observed :

> He is impersonally assigned by 'Government'—which is everybody, and more or less responsible to every ministry carrying on functions in his area. No ministry knows how much of his time it is entitled to, and none has any capacity for insuring that it receives that portion of his time and

9. For the hierarchical organisation of the State Secretariat, see Chart 4 : 1.

> energy. The result has been a halting and rather unclear removal of certain functions and personnal from his direct jurisdiction, but this arrangement involves in its own turn an interaction of the responsibilities and personnel of the ministries of health, education and agriculture, along with the home ministry and the ministry of finance, in association with the development and/or Community Projects Offices, and some lingering associations with the Collector. In a technical, administrative sense no one is really responsible for anything of much importance, and all share in responsibility for almost everything.[10]

In case of technical departments, there are other administrative units (known as Directorates) located outside the Secretariat. Besides Law and P.W.D., other technical departments are headed by the generalist Secretaries and consequently, there is a division of work between the generalist head and the specialist or technical head. The generalist head, i.e., the Secretary, looks after the general administration and advises the minister in the formulation of policy; the technical head looks after the technical affairs and is responsible for the implementation of policy as formulated by the minister. The technical heads are designated differently in different departments though 'Director' is the common designation. The relation between the generalist head and the technical or specialist head gives rise to the common debate—'Generalist versus Specialist' which is discussed elsewhere in this chapter. However, the technical head or the Director is assisted in his work by subordinate officers designated as Joint-Director and Deputy-Director. Below the Deputy-Director, there are generally Assistant Directors, who are area officers in-charge of areas functionally designed for administrative co-ordination. The technical departments have district officers posted at the district headquarters. They are designated differently in different departments, and head the

10. Paul H. Appleby, *Public Administration in India : Report of a Survey,* (New-Delhi : Government of India, 1953), p. 22.

units at the district level.[11] The Deputy Commissioner, as the administrative head of the district, is responsible for the co-ordinated functioning of the district offices of different departments.

Thus, we find that the hierarchical line of authority is intact and every officer is tied in a unified and single chain of command controlled by the Chief-Secretary and the Chief Minister through the departmental heads But a look at the hierarchy shows that, the number of posts become few and far between at the upper level. There is one to one relationship at the upper reaches of the hierarchy which results in excessive concentration and overloading.

Procedures of Work

Work in the government departments starts with the receipt of a communication in an office. The communication is first passed on to the dealing assistant after it is registered by a lower assistant. The dealing assistant provides relevant information in writing and passes it on to the next higher level, i.e., the Head Assistant or Assistant Superintendent or Superintendent as the case may be. In this way the file keeps on moving from table to table and from level to level for the disposal of business depending upon the nature and importance of the issue concerned and the dedication and interest of the officials. The government delegates authority to the Head of the Department who, in turn, issues guidelines and directives to subordinate officials for the disposal of the governmental business. The less important things are generally disposed of by the Superintendent or Under-Secretary. While disposing of the business, the officials generally tend to follow more the precedents, rules and regulations than to consider the importance and situational aspects of the cases. Rules are so complex and varied in nature that sometimes the disposal of an issue requires the concurrence of half-a-dozen departments

11. For the hierarchical organisation of a technical department, the P.W.D., see chart 4 : 2.

or branches which results in delay and, in extreme cases, kills the issue itself. Besides, everything in government departments is done in writing which not only multiplies the number of files and papers but also causes delay. This formal aspect of hierarchy—strict adherence to rules and regulations and written communication, being the method of work of the bureaucracy resembles Max Weber's conception of rational bureaucratic system.

The strict observance of rules and regulations and dependence upon precedents not only causes indeterminacy and delay but also creates confusion and discourages the spirit of initiative and enterprise which are of great importance in the administration of a country committed to the goals of nation-building and socio-economic change. This strict observance of rules and adherence to precedents by Indian bureaucracy has been considered to be a legacy of the colonial past.[12]

The complex and varied set of rules and regulations were introduced by the colonial rulers as a means of maintaining control over the large number of Indian subordinates with varying levels of training and outlook and who were dispersed far from the administrative centres.[13] After independence, not only the rules and regulations introduced by the colonial rulers were continued and multiplied but the rule-bound behaviour of the bureaucrats with self-defeating consequences also continued. "Too much adherence to procedure has a propensity of engrossing the whole individual. The repetitive acts yield psychological satisfaction and habits become ends in themselves and substitute for thought, instead of aid to thought. A cake of custom develops and hardens, hindering adaptation to changed circumstances".[14] Rules are based upon predictable occurrences and problems. But in the changing

12. Appleby, *op.cit.*, p.14.

13. Taub, *op cit.*, pp. 153-156.

14. A.R.Tyagi, *The Civil Service in a Developing Society*, (First ed., Delhi : Sterling Puplishers' Pvt. Ltd., 1969), p. 123.

environment of a developing nation, it is difficult to predict what the next problem will be. Thus the bureaucratic dependence upon rules and regulations "...may lead to preservation (that is, the continued application of the old rules, although they no longer cover the situation), or to the postponement of decisions, or to the passing upward of problems for increasingly higher level action. None of these responses is adaptive to the changing conditions that prompt them.... From the organisational viewpoint, they are dysfunctional, because they lead at best to delay, and at worst to a failure of communication and organisational self-evaluation".[15]

Organisational Incentives :

Promotion

Incentives play an important role in improving the efficiency, morale and performance of the employees in an organisation. 'Incentive' may be defined as an opportunity, attraction or encouragement to individual to do his best out of a hope of gain or fear of loss.[16] Unlike in other fields where profits are directly related to work performed, the problem of incentives in a public services is a difficult one.[17] Although, the formula of incentives applicable in private business organisations is not applicable in the case of public services, this does not mean that there is no incentives for good work in public services. In the bureaucracy, there are incentives for good work through increments, promotion, pension and recognition.[18] Here we shall discuss the system of promotion as a major incentive for improving efficiency and performance in the public services.

15. Taub, *op.cit.*, p. 157.
16. N. Murugesa Mudaliar, "Incentives in Public Service", *Administration and Politics in Modern Democratices*, ed., Sardar Patel Institute of Administration, Madras, (Allahabad : Chugh Publications, 1976), p. 243.
17. *Ibid.*
18. *Ibid.*

Promotion may be defined as a process which involves the assumption of higher duties and responsibilities by an employee accompanied by higher status and salary.[19] It covers both advancement between grades within the same class and between different classes.[20] The system of promotion and advancement affects not only the quality of the entrants to the Civil Services but also the efficiency of the administration as a whole.[21]

In Meghalaya, the principle followed in the case of promotion in class I services is merit-cum-seniority. Merit is judged on the basis of Annual Confidential Reports written for each officer by his immediate superior.[22] The Reviewing Officer offers his own remarks and may moderate or add to the remarks of the Reporting Officer. He further grades the officers into five categories: 'Outstanding', 'Very good', 'Good', 'Average' and 'Below Average'.[23] He also communicates the

19. C.N. Bhalerao, *Public Service Commissions of India : A Study*, (First ed., Sterling Publishers Pvt. Ltd., 1966), p.113.
20. In Meghalaya, the intra-service promotion i.e. from M.C.S. to I.A.S. has not yet been put into effect because the M.C.S. is yet to be recognised by the Government of India. The State of Assam and Meghalaya have a joint cadre of I.A.S. Hence, promotion to the I.A.S. has to be made from both the State Services i.e., A.C.S. and M.C.S. Since, M.C.S. is a new service, it needs to be recognised by the Government of India before making promotions of the M C.S. officers to the cadre of I.A.S. But after the creation of the state of Meghalaya, all Assam Civil Service Class II officers, who opted for Meghalaya, were upgraded to the M.C.S Class I as there is no classification in the case of the M.C.S. And it is because of this fact that the Govt. of Assam raised objection to the Govt. of India about the promotion of the M.C.S. officers to the cadre of I.A.S. on the ground that it would create dissatisfaction amongst both the A.C.S. Class I and Class II officers serving under the Government of Assam.
21. Tyagi, *op. cit.*, p. 255.
22. "AAP 28/59/1, 16-2-1959", *Handbook of General Circulars*, (Director, Organisation and Method Division, Government of Assam, 1965), p. 145.
23. *Ibid.*

adverse remarks, if any, to the officer reported upon;[24] one copy is attached to the officer's Confidential Report file and the other is sent to the Head of the Department of Service or the Secretary of the Ministry to which the officer belongs. Here it is filed after a review and counter-signature in token of accepting the remarks of the Reporting and Reviewing Officers; at this level, such modifications and additions in the previous remarks are made as are considered necessary.

Although, the rules for promotion in all services lay emphasis upon merit as the chief criterion, it cannot be said that there is a uniformity in the application of this principle; generally there is a hesitant synthesis of seniority and merit in different services. Whatever the extent of merit as a criterion, it is judged on the basis of the Confidential Reports in all services.

All promotions are ganerally decided by the government on the basis of the recommendation of a Promotion Committee,[25] the composition of which varies from service to service. The Public Service Commission is consulted in case of the promotion of those candidates who are recruited through the Public Service Commission. Though the Commission is consulted, its advice is not binding and sometimes promotions are made in utter disregard of its advice.[26]

However, the Promotion Committee considers the records of all the officers eligible for promotion which is twice the number of expected vacancies. First it excludes those who are considered unfit for promotion due to very adverse remarks.

24. *Ibid.*, pp. 148-149.

25. "ABI/27/57/4, 12-7-1957", *Handbook of General Circulars, op.cit.*, p. 104.

26. For instance of the non-acceptance of the Commission's advice, see the *Seventh Report of the Meghalaya Public Service Commission*, April 1, 1978 to March 31, 1979.

The Committee then grades all officers on the basis of confidential records. The list is prepared by placing the names in order of 'Outstanding', 'Very good', 'Good', without disturbing interse seniority within each category.[27] As a result, there is a scramble for 'Outstanding' categorisation because of the premium placed on it in the system of promotion and due to this any officer who is graded as 'Good' or 'Average' has very little prospect of promotion because those graded as 'Outstanding' and 'Very Good' supersede him.

The promotion system as a whole constitutes an important factor which may cause satisfaction or dissatisfaction amongst the bureaucrats, thus, affecting the efficiency, morale and performance of the bureaucratic organisation. This aspect of promotion will be discussed later in this chapter. It needs to be emphasized here that in order to be accepted by the employees, a promotion system should not only be fair and just but it should also appear to be so. Our study shows that in Meghalaya, personal, social and political influences pervade the promotion system in the public services. This is evident from the reports of the Union Public Service Commission and Public Service Commission of the Meghalaya State.[28] Frequently, promotions to higher posts are determined by political pressures and social connections. The factors of caste, tribe, religion, language etc., play a great role in promotion and act as a dampener on persons who do their work efficiently and are devoted to public interest. As Prof. Bhalerao has observed :

> The Civil Servants for being promoted must not displease his minister and important partymen. He has to keep proper relationship with his superior officer and his family.

27. "ABI/27/57/4, 12-7-1957," *Handbook of General Circulars, op.cit.*

28. C.N. Bhalerao, "Public Service Commissions of India : A Study", *op.cit.*, pp. 115-118.
See also the *Seventh Report of the Meghalaya Public Service Commission*, April 1, 1978 to March 31, 1979.

If he belongs to the same caste or sub-caste or comes from the same region as his superior officer, he may expect better chances of promotion. He must use the language which his boss understands and must be 'His Master's Voice'. To him, truth and fairplay are values subordinate to the goal of promotion. Promotions in Indian Public Services are thus frequently governed by political, social and personal considerations; this has led to a great deal of frustration among the public servants.[29]

Salary and Pay-Scales

The composition of an organisation is considerably reflected in the pay structure of its employees. A sound and uniform pay structure is a prerequisite of an efficient bureaucracy. It not only affects the tone and temper of the existing members of the bureaucracy but also has an important bearing upon the human material recruited to public services.[30]

In the Government of Meghalaya, there are at present 28 scales of pay divided equally between primary and secondary scales. The minimum basic salary for a lower official is Rs. 300/- per month whereas the maximum basic salary for the higher official is Rs. 2,500/- per month.[31] Thus, the ratio between the lowest and the highest pay-scale is 1 : 8.33 (pre-tax) and 1 : 6.33 (post-tax).[32] Besides, the super-time scale posts of the I.A.S. have salaries between Rs. 2,500/- and Rs. 2,750/- per month. These are basic salaries excluding special pay, dearness allowance and other compensatory allowances.

Even a casual glance at the existing pay structure in Meghalaya indicates that it is a relic of the colonial past. It appears that the pay structure is not based upon any rational

29. Bhalerao, "Public Service Commissions of India : A Study", *op.cit.*, p. 118.
30. Tyagi, *op.cit.*, p. 271.
31. *Report of the Meghalaya Pay Commission*, 1979, p. 16.
32. *Ibid.*

or well thought-out principle. With increase in prices and cost of living which affects all the people, a IV grade employee has to maintain his family with a salary of Rs. 500 per month, whereas an I.A.S. officer in the super-time scale receives a total salary of more than Rs. 3,000/- per month. Although there is no glaring disparity of ratio, there is no correlation between the salary of the higher and the lower level bureaucrats. It appears that the criterion on which the pay structure is based is the dignity and status of the posts and not the quantum of work performed.

Retirement

The case for retirement of public officials arises from the fact that after a certain age, mental and physical faculties tend to decline gradually, rendering the incumbents unsuitable for active service. Thus, the retirement system aims at increasing the efficiency in public services by eliminating the old and disabled bureaucrats and by injecting new blood and fresh ideas by recruiting the young and energitec persons in positions from which old bureaucrats have retired. The system also provides economic security to the bureaucrats and removes the temptation of bribery and corruption while in office. It further acts as a source of attraction for talented persons to join public bureaucracy.

The retirement age in case of public bureaucracy in Meghalaya is 60 years.[33] There is also the provision of pension after retirement and family pension to wife and dependent children in case of death.[34]

Informal Organisation

So far, we have discussed only the formal aspect of an organisation. Besides its formal aspect, there are also informal

33. *Report of the Meghalaya Pay Commission*, 1979, p. 32.

34. *Ibid.*, p. 37.

aspects which have a great impact on the nature and functioning of the formal organisation. Informal factors of organisations are an inevitable and universal feature of formal organisations. Man is by nature a social animal and it is his innate desire to live in company with his fellow beings. Unlike a piece of machinery, man has social needs,[35] which can be satisfied only through social relationships. The formal organisation itself provides a framework for social interactions among the individuals which significantly influence their behaviour and role performance. In an organisation, persons work together and come in contact with one another. From these contacts and collective working, there arise interactions between persons individually which are of a social nature.[36] From these interactions, there develop certain social relationships among individuals which have a decisive influence on the working of organisations.[37]

The personalised relationships based upon informal patterns of interaction form a basic part of the formal organisation. A study of the latter is incomplete without a study of the former because "you cannot understand an organisation or how it works from its organisation chart, its character, rules and regulations, nor from looking at or even watching its personnel. 'Learning the organisation ropes' in most organisations is chiefly learning who's who, what's what, why's why of its informal society'.[38] Recent studies like those of Peter M. Blau's *The Dynamics of Bureaucracy*,[39] have emphasized the importance of informal relationships in organisations.

35. Robert Dubin, *Human Relations in Administration*, (Third ed., New-Delhi : Prentice-Hall of India Pvt. Ltd., 1970), p. 28.

36. Barnard, *op.cit.*, pp. 40-41.

37. *Ibid.*, p. 114.

38. *Ibid.*, p. 121.

39. See Peter M. Blau, *The Dynamics of Bureaucracy : A Study of Interpersonal Relations in Two Government Agencies*, (Chicago : The Chicago University Press, 1963).

Informal relations are personal interactions based on know/ing each other as individual personalities belonging to different social groups and displaying spontaneity towards each other.[40] It refers to the unplanned, informal set of groups, friendships, and attachments that inevitably develop as a result of social attitudes, values and relationships when people are placed in regular proximity to one another.[41]

Such personal interactions which form the basis of informal relations may be formed within the office or outside the office. But basically such relationships emerge due to the formal interactions within the office.[42] These relationships may emerge due to a variety of reasons and have consequences on personal as well as organisational goals. To an individual, it may serve the function of providing a sense of security and also act as a mechanism for the outlet of strains and anxieties. Thus, it serves the function of tension management for an individual.[43]

In regard to the goal achievement of an organisation, the informal relationships may be positive, negative or neutral.[44] It is positive in relation to the goal achievement of the organisation in so far as it develops cooperation among the various members of an organisation and provides a social unit of framework within which agreement on working judgements and decisions are made. It is negative when antagonism dominates the outlook of members of an organisation and the relationship between them takes the form of a clique. It is neutral when the relationship between the members of an organisation is independent of their working relations and

40. Dubin, *op.cit.*, p. 118.

41. Arnold S. Tannenbaum, *Social Psychology of the Work Organisation*, (London : Tavistock Publications Ltd., 1971), p. 1.

42. Singhi, *op.cit.*, p. 113.

43. *Ibid.*, pp. 103-104.

44. *Ibid.*, p. 103.

focuses on pure socialibility as the reason for its existence. In other words, informal relationships may be functional or dysfunctional to the bureaucratic system.

In the following section, we shall study the informal relationships amongst the higher bureaucrats in Meghalaya, and we propose to classify these relationships under three separate headings, viz.: 'insiders and outsiders', 'generalist and specialist' and 'I.A.S. and non-I.A.S.'.

Insiders and Outsiders

To understand the informal relationships among the higher bureaucrats in Meghalaya in terms of 'insiders and outsiders', it is necessary to have some understanding of the general social features of Meghalaya because an organisation is a 'miniature social system'. The personalities and behaviour of individuals are moulded by social values and institutions. Society provides a web of values and expectations that determines the individual's character and his ethical beliefs.[45] The Meghalayan society, to-day, is broadly divided into two groups: 'insiders' and 'outsiders'. The membership of these groups is not based upon the place of birth or residence but community. Tribals are considered to be the 'insiders' i.e., the sons of the soil, whereas non-tribals, irrespective of their place of birth or residence, are considered to be 'outsiders'. This general feature of the society is also reflected in the bureaucratic system. The tribal bureaucrats are close to one another and form the group of insiders; the same is the case with regard to the non-tribal bureaucrats who constitute the group of 'outsiders'. The bureaucratic rank or hierarchical position does not stand in the way of relationship amongst the groups members. Irrespective of the form and extent of such relationships which are based on psychological, social and other such factors, the members of the groups are sympathetic towards one another. This sympathy is not limited

45. Robert Presthus, *The Organisational Society : An Analysis and a Theory*, (New-York : Random House Inc., 1962), p.7.

amongst the group members but extends beyond the group to the people who are to be administered. The bureaucrats are generally sympathetic to a client who happens to be the member of their own group and apply rules selectively. This aspect of the higher bureaucracy in Meghalaya has resemblance to what Fred W. Riggs calls the "bureaucratic elect" feature in his Prismatic-Sala-Model.[46]

The attitude of the members of the two groups towards each other is marked by resentment and lack of sympathy. The outsiders consider the insiders undeveloped and unsophisticated and not yet fit for doing the developmental work undertaken by government which requires initiative, skill and innovation. There are stories often told by the 'outsiders' of how tribal officials, being ignorant of rules and regulations, sought help from the non-tribal officials. Further, the 'outsiders' consider the 'insiders' incapable and inefficient who were recruited only because of their tribal origin. And as a result of the recruitment of such relatively less efficient tribal bureaucrats, the non-tribal bureaucrats consider themselves over-burdened with complicated and strenuous work which requires energy, sustained application and time, but without any reward. As one 'outsider' commented :

> I am given all the more complicated cases than those given to my colleagues (tribal officers) working in this court. The settlement of some of these cases requires time and energy which is four times more than what my colleagues devote. But our efficiency will be decided by the number of cases we successfully decide and not by the nature of the cases we are to decide.

Similarly, the outlook of the 'insiders' toward 'outsiders' is not a happy and favourable one. The 'insiders' consider the 'outsiders' self-seeking and not really interested in the develop-

46. Fred W. Riggs, *Administration in Developing Countries : The Theory of Prismatic Society*, (Boston : Houghton-Muffin Company, 1964), pp. 274-276.

ment of Meghalaya. They are interested in making money and administer without knowing or even understanding the problems of the state.[47] Almost 70.00 percent[48] of the tribal bureaucrats agreed with the statement[49] that the higher officials from outside the state did not understand the local problems and were not interested in developmental activities, while only 29.58 percent disagreed with it. The viewpoint of the officials who agreed with the statement is well expressed in the following comment of a tribal officer :

> How can the outsiders work for the development of the State ? Development requires first, the proper understanding of the problems and then, working with a heart full of sympathy for the area and the people facing the problems. The outsiders (both from within and without) do not and cannot understand the problems. The outsiders from without are transplanted here who do not know the ABC of our society. They are serving here because they want money at the end of the month and after retirement they will go to their homeland, and consequently, they do not bother about the development of the state. The outsiders from within are mostly from Shillong and their horizon does not extend beyond Shillong. As a result, they are also not acquainted with the Meghalayan society outside Shillong and, above all, they do not identify themselves with our society and always think in terms of Bombay, Madras, Calcutta, Delhi or other places where their

47. The same opinion prevails amongst a section of political leaders also. Emphasising the need of employing more tribals in the government jobs an ex-M.L.A. (sometime M.P. also) Shri Hopingstone Lyngdoh said "... I do not blame the outsiders; they must also get employment here or in their home state. I say that the distribution of responsibilities must be there and our people can look after our state in a better way. They will work not only for the sake of pay but also for their family, their state and their country". *See Meghalaya Legislative Assembly Debates,* Vol. VIII, No. 6, (Budget Session, 1974), p. 43.

48. See Table 4 : 1.

49. For the statement, See Appnedix C.

community men live. So the outsiders from within are also not interested in the development of the state.

On the other hand, the view point of the tribal officers who do not agree with the statement is well brought out in the comment of an officer who said :

> Development requires understanding of the problems and commitment to society. One can understand the problem provided one is sincere and committed to the task. The sincerity and commitment are the human qualities which can be possessed by any one irrespective of one's community. There are some outsiders who are really dedicated to the task of development and are sincerely working for it. They are generally in an advantageous position than we, the tribal officers, because they are not subjected to the same social pressures as we are and can work independently and impartially.

But what is surprising is that a considerable number of non-tribal officers i.e., 46.15 percent of the sample are in conditional agreement with the statement, while 48.72 percent disagreed and 5.13 percent remained neutral. The argument of the non-tribal officers, who disagree with the statement have similarity with their tribal counterparts that work for development does not depend upon the community of the administrators. On the contrary, it depends upon the interest and sincerity of the officers who work for development. And these qualities of interest and sincerity are human qualities, independent of caste, community and creed.

The bureaucrats who conditionally agree with the statement are of the view that it is not correct to say that the 'outsiders' do not understand the problems of the state although they are indifferent towards the state's development. The main reason they put forward for such an indifferent attitude is fear of insecurity. As one of them commented :

> How can I be interested to work for the development of

the state where I do not have any security ? I am working here but I cannot buy a plot of land of my choice because of the Land Transfer Act. In future, my relatives or friends from other areas would be unable to visit me at their will because of the proposed Inner Line Permit Bill. My children will not get a job here because of the reservation policy of the government. So, I cannot live here permanently. Circumstances will force me to go out after my retirement. My children will have to find out jobs outside the state. So, how will it affect me if the state remains undeveloped ? When I cross my age limit, I cannot find out another job. As I need money to feed myself and my family, I must somehow continue with my present employment, though I will continue it without much interest in it.

The government and the political parties are considered responsible for this wide-spread feeling of insecurity among the non-tribal officers. As a non-tribal officer said :

> The non-tribal administrators do not work for the development of the state, not because they do not understand the problems nor because of their lack of interest in developmental work but because they are suffering from a fear of future insecurity—a fear that is not limited to the non-tribal administrators alone. The whole non-tribal population in Meghalaya shares this fear and no one is certain about his future. This fear was not all along present here. There was a time when this area was considered to be the island of peace and tranquility in the troubled north-eastern region. But beginning from the sixties, the politicians and political parties started injecting a fear psychosis in the minds of the non-tribals, and, by late seventies, I think this fear has struck deep roots. If you go through the party manifestoes and speeches of political leaders during the period, you will find that they have blamed the non-tribal population for almost all the problems and scarcities (although this was not based on fact) and promised to

solve them in different ways.[50]

One thing that is strikingly common in the responses of both tribal and non-tribal officers who agree with the statement is that the outsiders are not interested in the development of the state. They attribute this to a lack of a feeling of belonging to the state and society. And this lack of feeling is the result of a lack of sympathy according to the 'insiders', whereas it is the result of a feeling of insecurity according to the 'outsiders'. Our findings regarding the 'insiders'-'outsiders' relationship raises a basic question faced by the higher bureaucracy in the state—which group of bureaucrats is equipped to implement the development plan ?

Besides, the division of the higher bureaucrats into the two resenting groups—'insiders' and 'outsiders', adversely affects congenial and co-operative relations among the members of the higher bureaucracy—a factor that facilitates communication and effectiveness.[51] Further, the fear of insecurity in the minds of a section of the higher bureaucrats causes frustration which does not permit them to work whole-heartedly for the development of the state. These are two important problems faced by the higher bureaucracy in Meghalaya which need serious attention by leaders and policy makers in Meghalaya.

50. It may be pointed out here that sometimes reference in the State Legislative Assembly goes against the confidence and morale of the bureaucrats, especially the non-tribal bureaucrats. As for instance, some members even criticised the communal composition of the higher bureaucracy in the state. Moving the no-confidence motion in the year 1975, Shri M. N. Majaw, leader of the PDIC (which was a partner in the coalition government of D.D. Pugh in the year 1978-79) attacked the government for having non-tribal I.A.S. officers in the top positions of the administrative hierarchy and demanded the immediate appointment of tribal officers in these positions. See Meghalaya Legislative Assembly Debates, Vol. X, No. 8, (the 2nd and 4th April, 1975), pp.99-100.

51. Appleby, *op.cit.*, p.19.

Generalist and Specialist

As we propose to discuss here the relationship between the 'Generalists' and the 'Specialists' in Meghalaya, we may start with working definitions of the terms 'generalist' and 'specialist'. The term 'generalist' refers to those officials of general educational background whose primary purpose is to assist and advise the ministers in the formulation of governmental policies and carry on general administration. The 'specialists', on the other hand, are those officials who are recruited to the public services on the basis of their specialised and technical qualifications and perform functions of a technical nature.

This aspect of the organisation, viz., the relationship between the generalist and the specialist came to the forefront and acquired great importance with the assumption of the welfare activities by the government. The changing balance in favour of welfare activities has compelled the government to accept greater responsibilities in the fields of science, technology and economic development. This is more so in a developing country where the public sector is better equipped to organise scientific resources to promote desired changes in social, economic, scientific and technological spheres.

In India, the administrative machinery has been dominated by the generalists since the British days. "Historically, the Civil Service in India has been designed as a generalist one with the leadership role at all levels and in all spheres of administration reserved for the Indian Civil Service, set up in 1854".[52] Although after independence, India continued the administrative system of the Colonial period unchanged and unbroken, the predominance of the generalists did not remain unquestioned. The specialists started voicing their discontent against the predominant role of the generalists as more and

52. Shriram Maheshwari, "The Specialist and the Generalist in Public Administration in India", *The Indian General of Public Administration,* Vol. XXI, No.1, (January-March, 1975), p.1.

more specialists were inducted into the different fields of the government service with the adoption of the system of planning in the early fifties.[53] The specialists were dissatisfied with the role traditionally set for them and a demand for change in the country's bureaucratic structure began together momentum. It was in this context that Prime Minister Mrs. Indira Gandhi said in 1967 :

> It is odd that the greatest doctors and engineers in the country, who would be rated as the leaders of the profession and who save lives or add permanent assets to the nation, can rarely hope to receive the pay or status of Secretaries of Ministers. The brightest of our young-men and women choose engineering and medicine. If they happen to go into government, they are very soon overtaken by the general administrator. This must change and I am trying to change it. The administrative system must reflect an individual's contribution to human welfare and economic gain.[54]

The dominant position of the generalists in administration and the need for technical specialisation for scientific, technological and economic development have led to the problem of relationship between the generalists and the specialists. The efficiency and effectiveness of the administrative system depends upon a solution to this problem and a recognition of their respective roles in the implementation of the country's developmental programmes.

Here we propose to discuss the relationship between the generalists and the specialists in the administrative system of Meghalaya, a proper understanding of which requires some knowledge about the status of the specialists in the administrative system of the state.

Meghalaya, like other states of the Indian Union, has a

53. *Ibid.*, p.3.
54. Quoted by Shriram Maheswari, *Ibid.*, p.4.

generalist-dominated bureaucratic system. In all departments, except Law and P.W.D., the generalists head the departments who advise the ministers in the formulation of policy. In the case of technical departments like those of Health, Public Health Engineering, Forests, Agriculture, etc., the generalists of the I.A.S cadre are the Secretaries. In such technical departments where Secretaries are generalist administrators, the specialists head the field units commonly known as Directorates and are designated as Directors. In some cases, the Director is also designated as the Additional Secretary to the Government (as in the case of the Director of Public Health Engineering who is also Additional Secretary to the Government). Even in some field units, the Director is a generalist administrator as in the case of the Director of Public Instructions who does not possess technical qualifications or experience in the field of education but is an officer of the I.A.S.

However, the specialists are subordinate in status to the generalist Secretary of a department and this is found to be one of the common causes of resentment among the specialists. They do not have direct access to the Ministers and consequently, they do not have direct share in the formulation of policy. The generalists advise the ministers in policy formulation; the specialists have voice in the process only through the generalist secretaries. Once the policy is decided, the specialists are consulted as to the best method of carrying out that policy. With regard to their pay-scales also, the specialists are in a disadvantageous and inferior position.

It is in this background that we studied the relationship between the generalists and the specialists in Meghalaya and found that this is one of the weakest links in the chain of bureaucratic relationship in the state. While commenting on a statement[55] about generalist domination, all the specialists

55. For the statement, see Appendix C.

without any exception[56] expressed their opposition to the present system. They branded the present system as 'amateurism of the generalist', and considered the present system as expensive and unproductive. What the specialists resent more is that sometimes a junior generalist with inferior academic background occupies a position which is higher in status and prestige than a senior specialist with a superior academic background. This according to the specialists, has a dampening effect upon their initiative and enthusiasm. The specialists strongly express the conviction that development work is bound to suffer unless the present system of generalist domination is ended. One specialist angrily commented :

> What to speak about the generalist domination ? Who would listen to us ? Our cry will fall on deaf ears because we are not to advise the Minister in making policy. After independence, we took up planning to make rapid changes in social, economic and scientific fields, the effective implementation of which requires a change in our administrative system. Unfortunately, the Colonial administrative system was continued without any substantial change in it. But this is unsuitable to a modern welfare state. In a modern welfare state, officials from every branch of administration must be given due share in the organisational set-up on the basis of merit, if the co-ordinated effort of all is to be enlisted for the implementation of welfare policies. Otherwise, the hope of an equalitarian society will be a distant dream.
>
> Look at the situation in Meghalaya. The specialists are not given recognition for their merit, technical specialisation, and seniority. For everything, they have to depend upon

56. In our sample we had specialists from three technical departments of P.W.D., P.H.E. and Health. Of these three departments, P.W.D., had a specialist as the Secretary. But even the specialists belonging to P.W.D. were opposed to the present arrangement in Meghalaya and drew attention to examples of illogical arrangements from other departments.

the generalist Secretary who is a layman without enough knowledge in the field (sometimes junior to the specialists also). This certainly has an adverse effect upon the initiative and drive of the experts who are considered to be the vehicles of scientific revolution. You cannot ignore the psychology of man. Psychologically a man gets depressed when he has to work under a boss who is not only junior to him but also inferior in ability....If you take the career pattern of the generalist and the specialist serving under Meghalaya Government, you will find that the career and ability of the specialists are superior to those of the generalists. For entering into the generalist administrative service, the academic qualification required is graduation from a recognised university, but to get admitted in an institution of medicine or engineering, one must have a bright academic career and a professional degree. But this career is finally considered inferior to that of a generalist as soon as one is in the Government Service. So, how do you expect us to be dedicated to the cause of society when we are not given our due ? How shall we maintain our initiative when we find that a man with equal career (sometimes inferior also) occupies a position which is higher in status as well as in pay.

The generalists on the other hand, are not unanimous in their views. A substantial number[57] of generalists does not find any fault in the present system and consequently ignore the question regarding the need for any change in the present set-up. They disagree with the charge that the specialists are not given their due share and defend the system on the ground that it is well-balanced. With regard to the formulation of policy, they are of the view that the specialists are consulted at some stage or other although ultimately, it is the Secretary (may be a specialist or a generalist) of a department who

57. 55.00 percent of the generalists, (44 out of 80) mostly from the I.A.S., A.C.S. and a few senior members of M.C.S. are of the view that the present system is alright.

advise the Minister. This is defended by them on the ground that 'generalisation' itself is a specialisation, and, above all, the technical aspect is only one aspect of a policy. Besides the technical aspect, the other aspects like social and political factors need to be considered and these aspects can be well-considered only by a generalist who has experience in diverse fields of administration. They justify their official status and salary on the ground that they are appointed only after qualifying themselves in a competitive examination of very high standard. Here specific mention may be made about a comment that was given by some generalists. While commenting on the low salary the 'specialists' receive in comparison to the 'generalists', they pointed out that extra sources of income (like medical practise by some doctors although they receive a non-practising allowance) were available to the 'specialists' which do not exist for the 'generalists'.

The other group of 'generalists' which holds a different view is surprisingly from the junior members of the State Services. They seem to be sympathetic towards the claim of the 'specialists' and recognise the need of some change in the present system although they expressed the difficulty involved in any such change. This group of 'generalists' does not consider the present system as a generalist-dominated one. To them, it is not a question of domination; it is rather a question of assignment of duties which goes contrary to the interest of the 'specialists', destroying their initiative and drive. They are of the view that there should be a unified civil service in the state instead of so many classes of services, as it will enable everyone to aspire for higher posts, depending upon one's merit. This will eliminate the feeling of deprivation and will make everyone work hard for being appointed to posts at the higher level, thus increasing efficiency in public administration.

Thus, it appears that while the specialists are aggressive towards, and dissatisfied with, the present system, the generalists have a defensive posture. The specialists reject the system out-right while the generalists defend the system although a group of them favours some change in the system. The generalists defend the system, as they do not want to have any encroachment on their position and authority. The other group of generalists, especially, the junior (State Service) group, is in favour of a unified Clvil Service because they are also the victims on account of so many classes of services. They defend their position against the 'Brahminic' attitude of their fellow colleagues belonging to the I.A.S. through the establishment of a unified Civil Service. The most disturbing element that appears here is the strained relationship between the 'generalists' and the 'specialists' which is detrimental to the effective implementation of development plans and programmes. For rapid development what is required is that both the generalists and the specialists must work in co-operation with one another and not in a strained atmosphere of mutual hatred and jealousy. But this spirit of co-operation and an understanding based on each other's role is substantially lacking in the relation between the 'generalists' and the 'specialists' and thus, is dysfunctional to the developmental goals.

I.A S. and Non-I.A.S. Groups

With the rapid development and expansion of the activities of government, there is a greater need for close co-ordination, co-operation and understanding among officers of different grades and services. In this context, it is interesting to study the relationship between the 'I.A.S.' and 'non-I.A.S.' officers serving under the Government of Meghalaya. This aspect of the bureaucracy in India is a unique feature and deserves special attention. After independence, we continued the parallel system of all India Services and the Provincial Services, a system that was created by the Britishers in order to maintain their hold on India while giving some concession to the Indian demand for more representation in the administration of the state. The all-India Services, namely, the I.C.S. was the repository of all powers during the British period and was composed of mostly the 'Ox-bridge' graduates of the middle class elite families of

England with a few Indians. The members of the I.C.S. occupied all key positions of authority and decision-making in the government and were considered to be the instruments of British imperialism in India. The Provincial Services were composed mostly of Indians and were subordinate to the I.C.S. not only in terms of authority, status and prestige but also in terms of pay and other service conditions. The system was continued after independence with the replacement of the I.C.S. by the I.A.S. and the Provincial Services by the State Services. Like its predecessor, the I.C.S., the I.A.S. is an all-India service, recruited and managed by the Government of India although there is no permanent cadre of the I.A.S. at the centre. The I.A.S. officers after recruitment are allocated to different states and serve the Central Government at one or other stage of their career on deputation. The I.A.S. has inherited much of the status and prestige of the I.C.S. and is considered to be superior to the State Services. The members of the I.A.S. occupy key positions in both the Central and the State Governments. The State Services, on the other hand, are managed by the State Governments and the officers of the State Services serve their respective State Governments. Their salaries and other conditions are determined by the State Governments and are generally much inferior to those of the I.A.S. These wide disparities in the conditions of service of the I.A.S. and the State Services have the effect of breeding 'superior' and 'inferior' class consciousness between them. In this connection, the following comment contained in the First Five Year Plan of Pakistan is relevant to the Civil Services in India :

> The existence of so many services of a general character as distinct entities divides the total general work of the government into watertight compartments, militates against the pooling of administrative resources, encourages class consciousness and mutual jealousness, creates conflicts in many common areas of administration and prevents the maximum utilisation of talents in accordance with aptitudes and emotional pulls, to mention only a few of the evils

resulting from it.[58]

In our study of the 'I.A.S.' and 'non-I.A.S.' officers in Meghalaya, we find that the relationship between them is one of the sources of strain in the higher bureaucracy in Meghalaya. The relationship between the two groups is not one of friendship but of mutual antagonism and jealousy. Both the group members are well aware of their status and there is no free mixing between the members of the groups. Undoubtedly, there are some exceptions here and there, but in general the relationship between the members of the groups is mostly regulated more by formal official procedures and less by informal code of conduct. The status differences are visible in their office equipment, secretariat assistance and in the degree of accessibility. An I.A.S. officer, senior or junior, is considered more important than his colleagues in the State Services and is not easily accessible to his subordinate or to the visitors. The status differentiation can further be marked in the quality of furniture and other such commodities that are available in the offices of the I.A.S. and non-I.A.S. officers.

And it is probably this awareness of status differentiation which injects a superiority complex in the mind of the I.A.S. officer, a factor which is agreed to by all the 85 'non-I.A.S.' officers in the sample. While commenting on a statement[59] all the 'non-I.A.S.' officers but one consider the superiority complex of the I.A.S. officers as unjustified, unfounded and counter-productive. These officers sharply reacted to the present system under which all higher positions in the government are virtually the monopoly of the I.A.S. officers.[60] An-

58. Quoted by S. Banerjee, "A Unified Civil Service", *The Indian Journal of Public Administration*, Vol.IX, No.2, (April-June, 1963), p.192.

59. For the statement, see Appendix C.

60. At the the time of the study all the posts of Secretary to Government except two were occupied by the I.A.S. officers. These two were Departments of Law and P.W.D. which were headed by a Lawyer and an Engineer, respectively. No officer of the

other source of discontent with the I.A.S. officer is their comparative young age and inexperience. Some 'non-I.A.S.' officers even went to the extent of saying that the I.A.S. officers are undemocratic and bear the stamp of imperialism. As one 'non-I.A.S.' officer said :

> The I.A.S. has its origin in the traditional I.C.S. which was the pillar of British imperialism in India. Our Constitution has contradicted the democratic ideal of state administration by providing for an all-India service whose members run the administration of the State. The I.A.S. inherited not only the structure from its parent body, the I.C.S., but also the behavioural and attitudinal features. The I.A.S. officers, like the I.C.S., consider themselves to be heavenly-born with superiority over all others. They consider the officers of other services as inferior to them. In a word, they consider themselves to be the rulers and masters of this country. This feeling of the I.A.S. results from their higher pay, time-bound promotion and, above all, their placement above the shoulders of so many senior officers of other services. This is not definitely in conformity with the maintenance of morale and self-respect of the 'non-I.A.S.' officers. The present system gives birth to a feeling of class and status consciousness and results in the lack of co-operation amongst different services which goes against the principle of sound and healthy administration.

The lone 'non-I.A.S.' officer who justifies the superiority complex of the I.A.S. officer is surprisingly an M.C.S. officer who was originally in the A.C.S. class II service. His argument was that the I.A.S. officers were undoubtedly superior in intellect and skill to the officers of the State Services.

On the other hand, 21 I.A.S. officers out of 25 did not agree with the statement that the I.A.S. officers live in ivory tower and look down upon officers belonging to other

State Services was found to be above the rank of Deputy Secretary.

services. They argue that in a hierarchical organisation, a certain status is associated with every level which moulds the attitudes and values of the officers belonging to that level and the I.A.S. officers are not an exception. They have the values and attitudes developed in them by their service which is considered to assume the form of a superiority complex by the 'non-I.A.S.' officers. But the people who call such values a superiority complex themselves are not free from the values and attitudes of their profession and service or a feeling of superiority complex in relation to subordinate colleagues.

The other four I.A.S. officers in the sample who were promoted from the State Services, hold a different view. They share the view-point of the 'non-I.A.S.' officers that the I.A.S. officers have a superiority complex and consider the officers of other services as inferior to them. It is to be noted here that these promoted officers occupy an inferior position in the hierarchy. Although they belong to the I.A.S. cadre, they are considered inferior by their fellow colleagues in the I.A.S. It is perhaps this which makes the promoted I.A.S. officers subscribe to the views of the 'non-I.A.S.' officers.

On an examination of the views of the 'I.A.S.' and 'non-I.A.S.' officers regarding the higher status consciousness and superiority complex of the I.A.S. officers, there appears to be an element of truth in the criticism of 'non-I.A.S.' officers against the I.A.S. officers. The simultaneous existence of so many services with varying service conditions in the same set-up creates class-consciousness, a consciousness which hinders co-operation among different units of the organisation. When development work requires a co-ordinated effort on the part of different units, "the existence of numerous special services and the absence of a unified and comprehensive public service exaggerates jealousies, rank consciousness and delay in cross-reference and other communication".[61] This aspect of higher bureaucracy is not a unique feature in Meghalaya but is a common feature of all the states of the Indian Union.

61. Appleby, *op. cit.*, p. 19.

However, from the above discussion it will be wrong to assume that the I.A.S. officer is a united and well-knit group, though apparently, it appears to be so. Even among the I.A.S., there exist sub-groups formed around caste, community, religion and language affiliations and political loyalties.

Job-Satisfaction of the Bureaucrats

After considering the informal relationships of the bureaucrats in the preceding section, we will now discuss the job-satisfaction of the bureaucrats in Meghalaya. The question of job-satisfaction occupies an important place in the study of organisations. Since much of the success of our development plan depends upon the bureaucracy, the bureaucrats' own perception and attitude towards their work-setting and their personal problems and the satisfaction they derive from their work of immense significance.

It is the job-satisfaction through which one expresses the way in which one is adjusting to his task and to his role within the organisation.[62] Although satisfaction is a psychological phenomenon and is subjective in character, varying from individual to individual,[63] we propose to study the job-satisfaction of the bureaucrats in relation to the nature of work, salary, promotion chances, status and prestige. As Arnold S. Tannenbaum said, "The responsibility, respect and recognition along with greater material rewards associated with status contribute significantly to the satisfaction of important needs and to a sense of self-esteem".[64] Status and self-esteem not only affect the satisfaction of organisation members but also their mental and physical health.[65]

62. Michael Crozier, *The Bureaucratic Phenomenon*, (New-Delhi : Eurasia Publishing House, 1975), p.22.

63. P.R. Dubhashi, "Satisfaction of an Administrative Career", *The Indian Journal of Public Administration*, Vol.XV, No.1, (January-March, 1969), p.110.

64. Tannenbaum, *op.cit.*, p.41.

65. *Ibid.*

But a study of the job-satisfaction of the bureaucrats by itself is not of much importance unless it is studied in relation to the motivation of the bureaucrats in joining their jobs. We made a brief study of the latter in the present investigation. In studying the factors that motivated the bureaucrats to join the public service, we asked them as to why they chose public service as a career, and found a wide variety of responses, which were classified into two groups : 'interested' and 'no alternative' group. We found 54.55 percent of the bureaucrats has joined the public service because they were interested in it, while 45.45 percent joined the public service because they had no other alternative but to join it.[66] If we analyse the responses of the two groups, we find that the responses of the interested group are uniform and simple. The members of this group joined the public service because they were attracted by the security, power, and social position provided by it. As one of them commented :

> What better career could be expected than a career in the Civil Service ? It provides security; not only security, but also power and prestige. With the rise in hierarchy, one gets more and more power to do good or bad. The public looks upon the highly placed Civil Servants with much awe and respect. So, when one has both money and power, one occupies a prestigious position in society.

What the bureaucrat said above represents the general Indian attitude towards the Civil Service. Civil Service had always a high place in Indian society, and the only lucrative avenue open to middle-class youth. Although, with scientific and industrial development, other fields have become as lucrative and, some of them even more than, the Civil Service, but the Civil Service, especially the higher one, has still enough glamour to attract the middle-class youth.

The responses of the 'no-alternative' category are not so simple as those of the 'interested' category. An analysis of the

66. See Table 4:2.

responses showed that some of the bureaucrats of this category did not have career planning. On the completion of their academic career, they were looking for jobs and got into the Civil Service. While others were trying for jobs other than Civil Service but having failed to secure them, they appeared in the competitive examination and got into the Civil Service. As an officer of the former category said :

> I did not have any plan about my career. The only plan I had was to find out a job after my examination, so that I could earn something and help my family. Accordingly, as soon as my examination was over, I was looking for a job and made application wherever I was eligible to apply. My list included posts from a clerical job in a business firm to a post in the Indian Administrative Service, and ultimately, I got into the M.C.S.

The above observation is a reflection of the condition of the middle-class youth in Indian society to-day. Most of the middle-class youth do not have any career plan or freedom to choose and go to educational institutions for obtaining a degree as a pass-port for competing in the job market. And the job-market being scarce, no option can be exercised. So, the entry into a job becomes a matter of chance unrelated to one's own aptitude or motivation.

However, the responses of the bureaucrats in the latter group highlight the problem arising out of the scarce employment opportunities in India. As one of the bureaucrats of this group said :

> I had the choice of scientific career but I failed to get one. I failed not because of my qualifications but because I did not have any links with the higher-ups. Thus, having no alternative, I had to join the government.

As our study of the motivation of the bureaucrats for joining the public service shows that a majority of the bureaucrats joined the public service because of its security, power and prestige, a question naturally arises : how far do the bureaucrats find these conditions present in the public service and how far are they satisfied with the conditions existing in the public service and with their work ? This question can be answered from the study of the job-satisfaction of the bureaucrats in relation to the nature of work, salary, promotion chances and status and prestige. For studying the satisfaction of the bureaucrats we asked a general question[67] and found different types of responses.

Nature of Work

In our study of the satisfaction of the bureaucrats with the nature of work, we found that 57.27 percent of the bureaucrats were satisfied with the nature of work while 42.73 percent were dissatisfied.[68] The reasons put forward for satisfaction with the nature of work include : interesting and challenging nature of work, scope for doing something concrete, and the responsibility that makes one feel important for the organisation. The reasons for dissatisfaction include such factors as : wrong placement unrelated to one's interest and aptitude, mechanical and routinised nature of the work and the complexity of rules and regulations which makes work difficult.

The dissatisfaction with the nature of work is expressed more by the technical bureaucrats than the non-technical bureaucrats.[69] While 37.50 percent of the non-technical bureaucrats are dissatisfied with the nature of work, the relevant percentage in the case of technical bureaucracy is 56.67. Again, among the technical bureaucrats, the dissatisfaction is more among the doctors than among the engineers. 60.00 percent of the doctors and 55.00 percent of the engineers are dissatisfied with the nature of their work. This widespread dissatisfaction among the technical bureaucrats is

67. For the question, see Appendix C.

68. See Table 4 : 3.

69. See Table 4 : 4.

mainly due to a lack of scope for the use of their specialised knowledge and training. As a doctor said :

> I find it very difficult to get any satisfaction from my work. If one is to be satisfied with one's work, one must have the scope for doing some useful work. But I find it very difficult to do any concrete work for which I am fit. Since I am a doctor, I am to do the work relating to medical profession. But here most of my energy is lost in writing letters and doing correspondence with so many departments. For doing a little bit of thing, I need to wait for month after month because there are hundreds of rules and regulations.

If we analyse the satisfaction of the bureaucrats according to their service, the I.A.S. tops the list of 'satisfaction with work'. While 76.00 percent of the I.A.S. officers are satisfied with the nature of their work ; the relevant percentage in the case of the A.C.S. and the M.C.S. is 60.00 and 55.00 percent, respectively. Thus, we may conclude that the higher the service more is the satisfaction with the nature of work.

Satisfaction with Salary

Salary occupies an important place in a bureaucratic system. It is the salary on which depends the standard of living that can attract capable persons to join public service. It is again salary which, to a great extent, determines the social status of a bureaucrat. Consequently, salary constitutes an important source of satisfaction or dissatisfaction of the bureaucrats.

In our study, we found only 30.00 percent of the bureaucrats to be satisfied with their salary while 70.00 percent are dissatisfied with it.[70] The common cause given for dissatisfaction is the high inflation rate and the fact that it has gone beyond their capacity to make both ends meet. While the

70. See Table 4 : 5.

value of money was falling, the salaries of the bureaucrats remained almost the same. One I.A.S. officer angrily burst out when he was asked to comment on his present salary. He said :

> How can you expect us to be satisfied ? You people look at the sum that an I.A.S. officer draws at the end of the month. Undoubtedly, this sum is three to four times more than what a clerk draws at the end of the month. But this is only one side of the picture. Our salary has not been increased proportionately to other services. The salary of clerk has increased by not less than 20 times during the last fifty years. But what is with us ? Our salary has remained almost the same. We are drawing almost the same amount that an I.C.S. officer drew fifty years back. But during these fifty years, the value of money has gone down by thousand times. So how can we be satisfied ?

Undoubtedly, a high inflationary rate is a major source of dissatisfaction not only among the bureaucrats but also among the people in general. The other reasons assigned for dissatisfaction with salary are more personal than general like family burdens and high aspirations.

The causes for satisfaction with the salary are found to be moderate aspirations, less family burdens and availability of family sources of income. And here we find a relation between economic background of the bureaucrats and the satisfaction with salary. Out of 33 bureaucrats in the 'satisfied' category, 20 are from the family of five thousands rupees or less annual income bracket, whereas 50 out of 77 bureaucrats of the 'dissatisfied' category have had an economic background of five thousand rupees and more per annum. Thus, the higher the economic background, less the satisfaction with salary, and the lower the economic background, more the satisfaction with salary. The reason for this is that a bureaucrat from a higher economic background has high aspirations which he cannot fulfil with his salary, and consequently, remains dissatisfied. A bureaucrat from a lower economic background has low aspirations which can be fulfilled with salary.

Again, the technical bureaucrats are found to be more dissatisfied with the salary than the non-technical bureaucrats.[71] 76.67 percent of the technical bureaucrats and 67.50 percent of the non-technical bureaucrats are found to be dissatisfied with their salaries. This higher rate of dissatisfaction among the technical bureaucrats can be attributed to the fact that the technical bureaucrats find themselves at a disadvantage in comparison with their fellow contemporaries in private organisations who earn much more and maintain a much higher standard of living than what the former do.

Among the non-technical bureaucrats, the I.A.S. officials are most satisfied followed by the A.C.S. and M.C.S. officials. 36.00 percent of the I.A.S., 33.33 percent of the A.C.S. and 30.00 percent of the M.C.S. are satisfied with their salaries. The higher rate of satisfaction amongst the I.A.S. officers can be attributed to the fact that their salaries and other service conditions are determined by the Central Government which are better than those of the State Services. The difference in satisfaction between the two State Services, namely, the A.C.S. and the M.C.S. may be due to the fact that the A.C.S. officers, by virtue of their seniority, occupy higher positions than those of the M.C.S. officers and, thus, they receive a salary higher than those of the M.C.S. officers. Furthermore, the annual increments of most of the M.C S. officers have been held-up for not being confirmed in the service due to the non-regulation of departmental examinations by the government,[72] and consequently, more M.C.S. officers are found to be dissatisfied with their salaries.

71. See Table 4 : 6

72. See the *Memorandum* submitted to the Chief Secretary, Government of Meghalaya by the Meghalaya Civil Service Officers' Association dated 19th March, 1979.

Satisfaction with the Promotion System

Promotion chances constitute another important source of satisfaction or dissatisfaction among the bureaucrats. Public bureaucracy is a hierarchical organisation in which the career of a bureaucrat is related to the avenues and chances of promotion available to him. Although, the methods and chances of promotion vary from service to service, the principle generally followed in case of promotions is merit-cum-seniority which has already been discussed in the first part of this chapter. Here, we shall study the satisfaction or dissatisfaction of the bureaucrats with the existing promotion system in Meghalaya. In the present study, we found that 44.55 percent of the bureaucrats are satisfied and 55.45 percent of the bureaucrats are dissatisfied with the method and chances of promotion.[73] The reason which the bureaucrats advance for their satisfaction is the objectivity of the promotion system, being based on merit and seniority. Seniority is a factor which cannot be tampered with and merit, mostly being judged on the basis of Annual Confidential Reports, is also, to some extent, free from subjective element. Although these bureaucrats express satisfaction, they point out that the chances of promotion are limited and that it is only after a long period of service that one is considered for promotion. Besides slowness and fewer chances of promotion, the other cause of dissatisfaction with the promotion system is its subjective nature. The dissatisfied bureaucrats object to the irrational and arbitrary way in which their performance is evaluated and Confidential Reports written on them. The major drawback of the promotion system, according to these bureaucrats, is that the superior reporting officers seldom make correct and objective appraisal of the performance of their subordinates. Often personal and social relationships, personal likes or dislikes of the officer, casteism, departmental factions and similar other considerations play an important role in the assessment made in the Annual Confidential Reports. One official commented thus :

73. See Table 4 : 7.

Promotion is made on the basis of Confidential Reports written by a senior officer. But the system of maintaining the Annual Confidential Reports is not an objective one and often fails to assess the quality of the officer reported upon. Sometimes the superior officer docs not know the subordinate officer on whom he is reporting and does not have any idea about the situation and conditions in which the officer is working. Besides, personal bias and prejudices for outweigh the merit and work of the officer reported upon. The reporting officer can write freely without fear of spoiling relations with the officer reported upon by making 'colourless' entry. Since the report is called 'Confidential', no officer can get to know how he is faring or being assessed unless he misses his promotion or appointment to a selection post. So, the officer has no protection in case of 'colourless' entries and consequently, it has come to be a generally accepted principle of promotion that the boss must be kept pleased even at the cost of duties.

If we analyse the satisfaction of the bureaucrats with the promotion chances in relation to the service to which they belong, we find that technical bureaucrats are more satisfied than the non-technical bureaucrats.[74] While 53.33 percent of the technical bureaucrats are satisfied with the promotion chances, the relevant percentage in case of non-technical bureaucrats is only 41.25. This difference in satisfaction between the technical and non-technical bureaucrats is due to greater and quicker promotion chances available to the technical bureaucrats because of the rapid expansion of technical departments and lack of technical qualified personnel in the State.

Among the satisfied non-technical bureaucrats, the I.A.S. officers are first in the list. 60.00 percent of the I.A.S., 40.00 percent of the A.C.S. and 30.00 percent of the M.C.S. are satisfied with the promotion system. Here again, it can be

74. See Table 4 : 8.

said that the I.A.S. officers are more satisfied because the promotion chances for the I.A.S. officers are brighter than those available to the officers of the State Services. In case of the I.A S., promotion is time bound. The least number of M.C.S. officers are satisfied with the present system of promotion because the promotion system in case of the M.C.S. has not been finalised and clearly laid out,[75] leaving considerable scope for arbitrary promotion. Further, no M.C.S. officer uptil now has been promoted to the I.A.S. cadre duc to the non-recognition of the M.C.S. by the Government of India.

Satisfaction with Prestige

Public servants enjoyed high prestige in the Indian society, especially during the British imperialist rule, when public bureaucrats were considered to be 'ma-baap' by the ordinary people. In our study of the motivation of the bureaucrats, prestige was found to be one of the motivating factors. Prestige is a complex interaction of many factors like pay, position in the hierarchy, authority to make decisions, power over others, contact with the higher-ups, various amenities available, and prestige in society.

In this study, a substantial number of bureaucrats, i.e., 61.82 percent were found to be satisfied with prestige.[76] The reasons advanced for their satisfaction are : power to do good or bad, control over the people, access to important personalities, and amenities available. 38.18 percent of the bureaucrats in our sample were dissatisfied and the reasons they put forward for this dissatisfaction are increasing democratisation, and a shift in the value system in society. One bureaucrat thus said :

No longer the government service has any prestige to-day.

75. See the *Memorandum* submitted to the Chief Secretary, Government of Meghalaya by the Meghalaya Civil Service Officers' Association, *op. cit.*

76. See Table 4 : 9.

The British days are over. To-day, people need not bother about the Civil Servant. They have direct access to the ministers who can get the bureaucrats in line with them. The standard of living of the Civil Servant has also gone. They are paid so poorly that they cannot follow the standard of living of their predecessors. Consequently, they are losing their position in society. Now, it is the business executives and the technocrats who have come to occupy the place of social elites. No longer, do the parents of prospective brides now look for a Civil Servant but for a business executive or a doctor or an engineer.

However, there is no marked difference in satisfaction between the technical and non-technical bureaucrats with prestige.[77] 61.25 percent of the non-technical bureaucrats and 63.33 percent of the technical bureaucrats were found to be satisfied with prestige. But if we analyse the satisfaction of the bureaucrats in relation to the service to which they belong, the I.A.S. is found to be the most satisfied group. 72.00 percent of the I.A.S. officers are satisfied with the prestige that is associated with their service. This is due to their superior position in the organisational hierarchy. This finding also confirms the general view that the I.A.S., like its predecessor, the I.C.S., is considered to be the most prestigious service by its members at least, if not by the society.

Summary

The efficiency of organisations is determined both by formal and informal factors. The formal aspect refers to the structural arrangement and frame-work of organisation which regulate the interaction and behaviour patterns of the functionaries working in an organisation. Therefore, the formal aspect of an organisation even if less important than its informal aspect, needs to be considered in a study of bureaucracy.

77. See Table 4:10.

The public bureaucracy in Meghalaya is hierarchically organised and linked by a chain from top to bottom. The work in this hierarchical system starts at the lower level and gradually keeps on moving to higher levels step by step. In the functioning of bureaucracy, rules, regulations and precedents are given more importance than the urgency and uniqueness of the issue under consideration which results not only in delay and sabotage of the issue but also detracts from the capacity of the organisation to adapt to new circumstances.

In the hierarchical chain, bureaucrats are promoted from lower level to higher level and the principle followed in case of promotion is merit cum seniority; merit being judged on the basis of Annual Confidential Reports. The Annual Confidential Reports are generally written without a proper sense of responsibility and are subject to personal likes and dislikes and social influences. Consequently, the system of promotion is generally considered defective, thereby adversely affecting the morale of the public servants.

The pay of the bureaucrats depends upon the service to which they belong and the position they occupy in the hierarchy. There are in all 28 pay-scales in Meghalaya having no co-relation between the pay of the lower and the upper levels of the hierarchy.

Apart from this formal aspect of organisation, there is also an informal aspect which is so much a part of the formal organisation that we cannot think of the latter without the former. Informal relations in organisations is an inevitable and universally existent feature of the formal organisation and have important consequences for the functioning of bureaucracy.

In a formal organisation, the functionaries interact with one another as members of different social groups and from these interactions, there develop certain relationships among them to satisfy their psychological and social needs. Caste, community, language, religion and common interest may act as the basis of such relationships and may sometimes take the form of formal groups within the bureaucratic sub-system.

The bureaucracy in Meghalaya is broadly divided into two groups i.e., 'insiders' and 'outsiders' on the basis of the area to which the bureaucrats belong. The relationship between the two groups is one of resentment which stands in the way of cohesion and effective co-operation and, thus, adversely affects the administrative system. Besides, a section of the outsiders is found to be indifferent towards the State and Meghalayan society as a whole. The indifference may frustrate the implementation of the programmes of socio-economic development of the state.

Within this broad classification of 'insiders' and 'outsiders', the bureaucrats may further be classified into the 'generalists' and the 'specialists' according to the nature of their functions. The top positions in the bureaucratic system are mostly held by the generalists which is one of the common causes of resentment among the specialist bureaucrats. This has developed a sense of deprivation among the specialists which may prove an obstacle to scientific and technological development in the state.

Again, there are antagonism and conflicts between the 'I.A.S.' and the 'non-I.A.S.' bureaucrats. The I.A.S., having its origin in the colonial service, the I.C.S., is a generalist service and occupies a secure position in terms of salary, status and career which is envied by other members of the bureaucratic system. This one-sided distribution of status and reward among a few deprive others who nourish a feeling of animosity and a sense of injustice in them. This status differentiation gives birth to a feeling of class-consciousness among the members of different services impairing their 'esprit de corps' and co-operation and, thus, obstructs the process of rapid development.

The effective functioning and goal achievement of an

organisation depends upon the people who man the organisation. And the efficiency of the functionaries to a great extent is influenced by the satisfaction which they derive from their work and organisation. In other words, job-satisfaction is an important dimension in the study of a bureaucratic system. But to make the study of job-satisfaction meaningful, it must be studied in relation to the motivation of the bureaucrats for joining the service since motivation and job-satisfaction are related to one another.

Though a great majority (i.e., 54.55 percent) of bureaucrats in the sample were found to be motivated to join public service, in case of job satisfaction the process is just the reverse. About the satisfaction of the bureaucrats with different aspects of the job, we found the largest number of bureaucrats to be satisfied with the nature of work and prestige while the least number of bureaucrats were found to be satisfied with salary and promotion chances. The least satisfaction with salary and promotion chances reflects the concern of the bureaucrats regarding their material needs and career.

Regarding the nature of work and salary, the non-technical bureaucrats are found to be more satisfied than the technical bureaucrats. But regarding promotion chances and prestige, technical bureaucrats are found to be more satisfied than the non-technical bureaucrats.

However, in terms of service of the bureaucrats, we find the I.A.S. at the top of the list of satisfaction with the different aspects of the job. This indicates one-sided distribution of status, position, prestige and rewards among a few, thereby creating a wide gap between the different services. This creates a sense of deprivation in the minds of the bureaucrats and, consequently, there is animosity, jealousy and frustration. The pace of development in the state is bound to be slow because of the lack of co-operation and cohesion among the members of the higher bureaucracy.

5

Bureaucrats and Politicians

In the previous chapters, we studied the factors relating to bureaucrats as individuals and those relating to the organisation in which the bureaucrats function. But the study of these two dimensions alone is not enough to understand the role of bureaucracy in development. As Prof. Ramashray Roy aptly says :

> ... the factors relating to the administrators as individuals and those relating to the functioning of the administrative system alone will not give us a complete understanding of the role of bureaucracy in...development. We need to know the nature of interaction between the administration and the environment it operates in. In this process of interaction the organisation has to contend with the operational limitations the environment imposes on the desirability as well as on the feasibility of certain actions proposed or undertaken by the organisation.[1]

1. Roy, *op.cit.*, p.20.

Thus, the study of bureaucracy is not complete without a study of its environment in which the bureaucracy functions. Though the study of bureaucratic environment has a number of important inter-related dimensions, the present study will be limited to the political environment because it is the political leaders who determine systemic goals in a democratic system and direct the operation of government and administration. And the goal realisation of the system is dependent upon the proper relationship between the political leaders and the bureaucrats, and the exploration of certain critical dimensions of their relationship is central to any enquiry about bureaucratic performance.[2]

In this chapter, we shall study the various kinds of pressures exerted upon the bureaucrats by the politicians and political leaders and the way the bureaucrats deal with these pressures. We shall also study the consequences of these pressures upon the bureaucrats as individual and bureaucracy as an institution designed to serve the goals of nation-building and socio-economic change.

To gain a clear understanding of the problem posed above, it is necessary to start with the politico-bureaucratic relationship in India in its historical context. The bureaucracy in its modern form was established in India by the Britishers and it was with the help of bureaucracy that the Britishers maintained their hold in India. During the British period, the bureaucracy was not subject to political control and a bureaucrat was accorded full protection to sustain his authority as the pivot of colonial administration. Although the Governor-General was at the helm of affairs and was vested with the power of supervision and control, he was not given the authority to initiate disciplinary action against a delinquent bureaucrat. That power was reserved with the Crown exercisable through the Secretary of State for India. Secure within this framework, a bureaucrat had little or no problem in assisting the government with diligence, probity and to the best of his ability. But

2. *Ibid.*, p.82.

such a role of the bureaucrats was resented by the political leaders in India. To the political leaders, the bureaucrats were the agents of foreign imperialist rulers, working in the interest of foreign power at the cost of national interest. They were critical of the bureaucratic machinery and had a feeling of suspicion, distrust, and hostility towards it. But after the achievement of independence in 1947, there took place a radical change in the situation. With independence, we adopted the parliamentary system of government where the bureaucracy had to function under the direction and control of the political leaders. The politicians, after independence, found the bureaucracy as the only instrument available to them in their programmes of development and the bureaucrats, on the other hand, had no other alternative but to accept their new role of functioning under political direction.

Moreover, the achievement of independence and the adoption of democratic and parliamentary form of government have changed the role of both the politicians and the bureaucrats. The role of the politicians has been changed from organising agitation to managing the affairs of the state, and operating government and fulfiling peoples social and economic aspirations and demands. The bureaucrats, on the other hand, are to come down to the people, not with the idea to rule, but with the idea to serve, and in this task of service they are to be guided and directed by the political leaders. Herein lies the importance of the relationship of mutual trust, understanding and co-operation between the political leaders and the bureaucrats. But how far such relationship of mutual trust and understanding has developed in India is a matter of anybody's guess. If the accounts given by the national dailies and the public discussions are of any indication, then it can be said that such relationship of mutual trust and understanding has not only not developed in India but also worsened.[3] Frequently, it is found that ministers and political

3. On this subject, see the recent letter by Shri A.K. Chatterjee, a senior officer of the Bihar cadre of the I.A.S. addressed to the Cheif Minister of Bihar, reproduced in Appendix D.

leaders, when faced with the criticism of poor performance, generally blame the administrative machinery and civil servants who cannot defend themselves in the legislature.[4] The bureaucrats are made a scapegoat by the politicians, press and the society in general. As Prof. Subramaniam writes:

> Too often, there is a tendency on the part of the political leaders to be contemptuous about the role of the Civil Servants. Too often also, there is a tendency on the part of the interested sections in the press to paint the image of the Civil Service and the political system in lurid colours. Sensationalism and scandalising are the order of the day. Good, honest work, amelioration of distress, and positive achievement in welfare administration do not get any recognition in the press whereas minor deviations from established procedures are magnified beyond all proportion. Official arrangement for propaganda are treated with scorn and the press... plays to the gallery to get cheap popularity by contemptuous comments on administration and securrilous attacks against the political and administrative executives. The same is true in the references made to the services in Parliament and in the State Legislatures. The Civil Service ought to be nameless and faceless so far as legislature is concerned, but it is a matter of disappointment that in this country, ill-informed and irresponsible criticism of the Civil Service, which is not in a position to answer back, is indulged in the legislatures. Parliamentary and Legislative immunity are excellent principles but our democracy must also learn that irresponsibility and impunity in criticism of administration is likely not only to lead to a weakening of initiative and to develop frustration among the administrators but also to ineffectiveness in the political system to translate the ideals of democracy into practice.[5]

4. P.V.R. Rao, *Red Tape and White Cap,* (First ed., New Delhi : Orient Longman Ltd., 1970), p.8.
5. V. Subramaniam, "Role of Civil Service in Indian Political System," *The Indian Journal of Public Administration,* Vol.XVII, No.2, (April-June, 1971), p. 262.

Similarly, G.D. Khosla, a reputed ex-civil servant, presents an alarming and distressing picture of the state of affairs regarding the relation between political leaders and civil servants in the following words:

> I have spent no less than fifty years in various departments of the Establishment, and I have been associated with hundreds of civil servants. I have a deep and enduring feeling for them, and I am grievously pained to see them collapsing and disintegrating under the incessant buldgeoning [sic.] of self-seeking politicians. 'They are corrupt. They are arrogant. They are power hungry. 'They are unpatriotic, reactionary, obstructionist, and they are (the Devil take them) disloyal'.
>
> When I survey the administrative scene I find it barren of ideas (where is the time to sit down and think when you have to dance attendance on these morons ?); the old dedication and efficiency vanishing (chaltahai); a total lack of initiative (why should I stick my neck out ?); integrity and probity mere shadows of their past reality (what is there in it for me ?) ; and a general overall flabbiness (I am trying to be loyal).[6]

Though the above mentioned quotations from V. Subramaniam and G.D. Khosla indicate the nature and extent of political pressures upon the bureaucrats, they are not something unique to India or Meghalaya. They are an inherent feature of the democratic system and are all-pervasive in administration in all developing countries.[7] In a democracy, two sets of functionaries with different training and attitudes need to function in close co-operation with one another. One set of functionaries is that of the politicians and political

6. G.D. Khosla, "Civil Servants Dilemma : Salvaging a Noble Legacy", Statesman, (Calcutta), September 3, 1980.

7. For a vivid picture of political pressure upon the bureaucrats in a developing country see Ataur Rahman Khan's, *Ozaratir Du Bachhar* (Two Years of Ministry), Dacca : Naoroj Kitabistan, 1972).

leaders, the other set being that of the bureaucrats. The bureaucrats are the permanent executives who, by habit and training, are required to judge the merit of particular cases in the light of impersonal and universal standards that are already laid down for their guidance. The politicians, on the other hand, are not the permanent executives. They are not selected but elected and for getting elected, they depend upon the verdict of the people. Since their future depends upon the people, they spend a substantial amount of money, time and energy in nurturing their respective constituencies and the people whose verdict they seek from time to time in order to continue in power. For nurturing the constituency or keeping the people satisfied, the politicians must bestow some favours (may be legal or extra-legal) on the people or at least on their supporters in the constituency. But the politicians by themselves cannot bestow any favour directly. In doing this they depend upon the bureaucrats and consequently, they put pressure upon them. This poses a dilemma for the bureaucrats because if they stick to rules and regulations, they are bound to create dissatisfaction in the minds of the clientele and invite displeasure of the politicians who are in a position to take revenge on them. On the other hand, if they depart too much from the bureaucratic rules and regulations and succumb to such pressure, legal rational criteria of bureaucracy will be sacrificed, resulting in"... highly personalised administration creating in its wake a situation where favouritism, power considerations, and extra-organisational criteria are likely to influence the decision-making process".[8] This will endanger the organisational viability of the administration as well as its goal achievement.[9]

After a discussion of the nature and mechanics of political pressures and influence on the administration in general, an attempt is made in the remainder of the chapter to study the political pressures which operate on the higher bureaucracy in Meghalaya. In studying political pressures, a number of

8. Roy, *op. cit.*, p. 80.
9. *Ibid.*, p. 97.

questions need to be answered : How frequently do the politicians exert pressures upon the bureaucrats ? What are the various types of pressures ? What are the possible consequences a bureaucrat has to face if he does not submit to pressures ? How does a bureaucrat deal with political pressures ?

For a study of the frequency of political pressures, a question regarding the operation and frequency of political pressure[10] was asked to the bureaucrats and it was found that none of the bureaucrats denied the operation of political pressures, although they differed in identifying the degree of frequency. While 34.55 percent of the bureaucrats consider political pressures to be very frequent and frequent, 19.09 percent of the bureaucrats consider them to be less frequent and 11.82 percent consider them to be least frequent.[11] As a whole, in our study, 69.10 percent of the bureaucrats find high frequency of political pressures. Another thing to be noted here is that bureaucrats working in the field consider political pressures to be more frequent than the bureaucrats working in the Secretariat or headquarters. The bureaucrats working in the headquarters are engaged in policy formulation and not policy implementation, and consequently, they are relatively free from political pressures. The task of policy implementation is vested in field units and, hence, they are more pressurised by the politicians. In this study, no marked difference is found between the responses of technical and non-technical bureaucrats about the frequency of political pressures.

However, a question that arises here is : for whom do the politicians exert pressures upon the bureaucrats ? Do they seek their own interest or the interest of their supporters or of the people of the constituency in general or of all the three ?

In a democratic set-up, politicians being the representatives

10. For the question, See Appendix C.
11. See Table 5 : 1.

of the people, are expected to look after the interests of the people whom they represent. This is the universalistic norm followed in a democratic set-up. But politicians, being human, may deviate from this universalistic norm and may follow the particularistic norm i.e., they may seek only their own interests or the interests of their supporters, friends and relatives. But how frequently do the politicians deviate from this universalistic norm ?

In order to study this aspect of political pressures, we asked a question[12] to the bureaucrats about the nature and frequency of demands the politicians made upon the bureaucrats. An analysis of the responses[13] to this question shows that politicians most frequently approach the bureaucrats with the demands of their supporters. This is not surprising because in a democratic set-up politicians must keep their supporters satisfied in order to be in power or to come to power. It is with the help of the supporters only that the politicians can make headway in electoral politics.

However, in the frequency distribution next to the demand of the supporters, we find the demand of the relatives and friends, the demands of the people of the constituency and lastly the demands concerning the politicians' personal interests and the interests of the members of their family are pointed out by the bureaucrats. Though the demands concerning politicians' personal interests and the interests of the members of their family stand last in the frequency distribution, it is widely considered that politicians in Meghalaya do follow particularistic norms and pursue parochial interests. On the basis of the data presented in table 5 : 2, it can safely be asserted that the politicians in the State tend to pursue parochial interests both for themselves and others, and accordingly, frequently pressurise the bureaucrats in either furthering or safeguarding such interests.

12. For the question, see Appendix C.

13. See Table 5 : 2.

Types of Political Pressures

After studying the nature of demands the politicians make upon the bureaucrats, the next question is : how do the politicians pressurise the bureaucrats? Do they themselves approach the bureaucrats to get done what they want or do they approach them through some other functionaries ? It would be of considerable significance to study the ways and means followed in exerting political pressures upon the bureaucrats, and for studying this aspect, we asked the bureaucrats to identify the important ways through which politicians exerted pressures upon them. The question elicited a wide variety of responses which we classified into six categories :

1. Making approach through the political leaders at the higher level (M.L.A., M.D.C., Minister, etc.)

2. Making approach through administrative officers at the higher level.

3. Persuasion through administrators' friends or relatives.

4. Threat of consequences for non-compliance.

5. Promise of better career opportunities to bureaucrats.

6. Pressure through demonstrations like gheraos, dharnas, etc.

It is clear from the aforesaid categories of responses that in the case of the first three categories, pressure is brought upon the bureaucrats not directly but indirectly ; whereas, in the case of the last three categories, pressure is brought upon the bureaucrats directly by the politicians themselves. An analysis[14] of the responses we received reveals that indirect political pressures account for 84.73 percent of the responses

14. See Table 5 : 3.

while direct type of pressures account for 15.27 percent of the total responses.

Among the indirect types 'making approach through political leaders at the higher level' accounts for the highest percentage of responses (38.17 percent) followed by 'approach through administrative officers at the higher level' (30.53 percent) and 'persuasion through administrators' 'friends and relatives' (16.03 percent).

Among the direct types of pressures, 'threat of consequences accounts for 6.87 percent of the responses followed by promise of better career opportunities' and 'pressure through demonstrations like gheraos, dharnas, etc.' which account for 6.11 and 2.29 percent of the responses, respectively.

Thus, we find that making approach through political leaders at the higher level is the most commonly used type of poli. tical pressure upon the bureaucrats. This is obvious as politicians are closer to the political leaders who are easily accessible to them. The political leaders are dependent upon the local politicians for their political strength. Consequently, the political leaders, for keeping their political support base intact, try to fulfil the demands of the politicians. This finding corroborates our earlier finding in this chapter that politicians frequently approach the bureaucrats with the demands of their supporters (according to 61.82 percent of the bureaucrats).

Pressure through political intervention may follow different forms of approach. As a bureaucrat commented :

> For getting something done from the administration, the politicians contact the political leaders at the higher level who bring pressures in many ways. Starting from telephone call or recommendation on an application, there may be personal visits and pressure may be in the form of request or order depending upon the rank in the hierarchy wherefrom the order comes.

In this connection, we may refer to an instance cited by A.D. Gorwala in his *Report on Public Administration in India*. In his *Report*, Gorwala pointed out that an M.L.A. made a request to the Collector of a District. The M.L.A., on enquiry, was informed by the Collector that his request could not be entertained because it would detrimentally affect other people. The M.L.A. telephoned the Minister from the Collector's chamber and informed the Minister that his request was not accepted. The Minister phoned back the Collector and told him that what the M.L.A. had asked for should be done. The Collector wanted to argue but the Minister ended by saying "well you know my views. You can do what I want or...."[15]

Political Pressures and the Bureaucrats' Dealings with them

From the above discussion, it is clear that political pressures and influences operate extensively in the administration, making the position of the bureaucrats delicate and difficult. If the pressure is exerted for legitimate demands, the bureaucrats do not find much difficulty. What they need to do is only to speed up the matter. But if the pressure is for some illegitimate demands or irregular purpose, the bureaucrats find themselves on the horns of a dilemma and it would be interesting to study how do the bureaucrats deal with such dilemma.

In this study, the bureaucrats were asked to identify the important courses they generally adopt when political pressures are exerted upon them.[16] The responses we received can be classified into seven categories :

1. Express inability because of rules and regulations.

15. A.D. Gorwala, *Report on Public Administration*, (Planning Commission, Government of India, 1951), pp. 23-24.

16. For question, see Appendix C.

2. Try to deal with the situation themselves but by seeking support from the higher level bureaucrats so as to avoid risk.

3. Refer the case to the higher-ups.

4. Try to deal with the situation themselves but by seeking support from the higher level political leaders.

5. Deal with the situation themselves.

6. Seek transfer to some other place.

7. Appeal to the good sense of the politicians.

A detailed study of the responses reveals that the bureaucrats follow two courses of action when subjected to political pressures. Firstly, they try to express their inability due to existing rules and regulations and appeal to the good sense of the politicians. Secondly, the bureaucrats either push up the matter or deal with it by seeking support either from higher level bureaucrats or political leaders, so as to avoid risk. There may be two reasons behind the seeking of support from the higher authority. Firstly, if anything goes wrong with a bureaucrat's decision, then he alone cannot be held responsible for that; and secondly, the dissatisfied politician cannot take retaliatory measures against him without the support of higher level authority who has already been consulted by the bureaucrat in arriving at his decision.

An analysis[17] of the responses shows that 27.98 percent and 2.98 percent of the responses account for the first (express inability) and seventh (appeal to the good sense of the politicians) courses of action respectively as listed above. The course of dealing with the situation themselves but by seeking support from the higher level administrators accounts for 23.83 percent of the responses, while the course of dealing

17. See Table 5:4.

with the situation themselves but by seeking support from the higher level political leaders accounts for only 14.93 percent of the responses. Thus, we find that bureaucrats, confronted with political pressures, prefer to apprise more the administrative superiors than the political superiors. This is because a bureaucrat is closer to his bureaucratic superiors than to political leaders. Besides, a bureaucrat can understand the difficulties of another bureaucrat better than what a political leader can do.

Again, the percentage of responses (22.39 percent) for the course of 'referring the case to the higher-ups' shows that there is a process of what is called 'upward deference'. This upward deference takes place because of the anxiety which is one of the most compelling human drives. Anxiety appears when something threatens the individuals' relations with persons important to him.[18] Political pressures cause anxiety in the minds of the bureaucrats as it threatens their relationship with the political leaders and the politicians. "The mechanism used to reduce anxiety" according to Robert Presthus "includes avoiding responsibility by dependency upon one's superiors". This is done generally by forcing the task upward in the hierarchy, so that all responsibility for their performance may be disclaimed. But this is often dysfunctional to the organisation because it reduces the ability to handle anxiety realistically.[19] Moreover, the process of upward deference also results in the congestion of work at higher level of the hierarchy causing inefficiency and delay.

Consequences of Unfavourable Response to Political Pressures

What are the consequences if bureaucrats fail to meet the demands of politicians and to respond favourably to political pressures and influences ? For studying this aspect, we asked

18. Presthus, *op.cit.*, p.104.

19. *Ibid.*, p.106.

the bureaucrats to specify important consequences that follow their failure to meet the demands of the politicians.[20] The answers received were grouped into four categories :

1. Their service will be adversely affected by transfer, complaint to higher authorities, etc.

2. Co-operation from the politicians will be lacking.

3. Their service records will be spoiled.

4. They will be subject to public denigration, or criticism.

An analysis[21] of the different categories of responses reveals that the consequence of 'adversely affecting their service by transfer and complaint to higher authorities' is the most frequently-named consequence which alone accounts for 37.45 percent of the total responses. Transfer is one of the most important means available to the political leaders for punishing a bureaucrat.[22] In a democratic system, transfers and postings of higher bureaucrats are mostly determined by the political executive, but this is not always done on the basis of merit. In some cases, purely political criteria determine the posting of higher bureaucrats. While answering an Assembly question the Chief Minister of Meghalaya himself confessed a case of transfer under political pressure.[23] However, transfer under political pressure is not something unique in Meghalaya. It is the usual practice followed by the politicians in different states and different political systems to pressurise the upper echelon of political hierarchy to get an officer transferred if they do not get along with him. Thus, a

20. For question, see Appendix C.
21. See Table 5:5.
22. For a vivid picture of how politicians try to have a non-complying administrator transferred, see Ataur Rahman Khan's *Ozaratir Du Bachhar*, (Two Years of Ministry), *op.cit.*
23. *Meghalaya Legislative Assembly Debates*, Vol.III, No.2 (Winter Session, 1972), p.34.

writer has quoted a minister named Kroma as saying to a young I.A.S. officer about one of his colleagues named Avasthi: "People of your service are good; but very difficult to get along with. Look at Avasthi. He is so honest and competent and upright, but he is no use to us—whenever I ask for something, he opens the book. I shall have to get him transferred, if we have to win the election."[24] Similarly, about the Civil Service of Pakistan Goodnow wrote:

> If the officer went along with the request, the favour-seeker would see that the officer was praised at the right time and in front of the right people. If the officer stuck to his principles and refused the request, pressures were applied at the political level to have him transferred to another—perhaps much undesirable post.[25]

Transfers under political pressure are a common feature of personnel administration in every state in India, adversely affecting the morale of the administrators and the efficiency of the administrative system. Transfers, especially forced transfers, cause a lot of personal inconvenience and difficulties to a public servant and, consequently, they undermine the honesty and the integrity of the public servants. This point was well brought out in the comment of an administrator in our sample who said:

> Officers are not solely responsible for the lack of honesty and integrity in the public service. It is the system which sometimes makes an officer dishonest. If an officer is honest and follows the ethics of Civil Service and does not cow down to the political demands he will have to suffer a lot. Instead of being rewarded, he will be subjected to harassment. One of the methods to harass an officer is to transfer

24. Quoted by Anon "Transfer of the Collector of Matsyapura", *New Challenges in Administration*, ed., Committee on Case Studies, (New-Delhi : Indian Institute of Public Administration, 1972), p.8.

25. Goodnow. *op.cit.*, p.236.

him to the interior, so that he gets a lesson. The education of his children will suffer, financial burdens will go up. All these are the rewards for his honesty and integrity...and make the officer feel that honesty and integrity are hollow words.

Besides leading to frustration, frequent transfers of an officer under political pressures prevent him from gaining mastery over his job and do not permit him to execute his tasks fully.

The other consequences which result from the non-fulfilment of political demands, 'lack of co-operation' accounts for 29.96 percent of the responses, 'spoiling service records' accounts for 20.60 percent of the responses, and 'public denigration and criticism' accounts for 11.99 percent of the responses.

The lack of co-operation from the politicians seriously hampers the goal achievement of the organisation. The desired national goals in a democratic system cannot be achieved by the bureaucratic structure unless it is supported by the political structure. The implementation of the goals of nation-building and development depends upon the co-operation between the politicians and the bureaucrats. While the bureaucrats implement the authoritatively-determined development programmes, the politicians articulate and aggregate public demands and mobilise public support for the programmes. So long as this co-operative relationship does not exist, the development programmes are bound to suffer.

The other consequences of 'spoiling the service records' and 'public denigration' also affect the functioning of bureaucracy. While spoiling service records makes the bureaucrats hostile towards the politicians and governmental programmes, public denigration undermines self-confidence, and the spirit of enterprise-qualities which are essential for development administration. Analysing the administrative weaknesses in

India, H.V.R. Iengar, an eminent ex-Civil Servant, said:

> As a result of certain recent events, the impression has been created that the structure which we adopted from the British, namely, a Civil Service which is non-political and which can serve a government of any complexion and is able to preserve continuity and tradition, has no longer any validity. Civil Servant no longer feel that they will be protected by their Ministers against attacks in Parliament. The consequence of all this is a slowing down in the whole process of decision-making, a reluctance to take bold decisions and a tendency to "pass the buck" around as far as possible.[26]

Summary :

Bureaucracy does not operate in a vacuum but in close interaction with society and the political system of which it is a part. In this process of interaction, the bureaucracy has to work within the operational limitations the environment imposes upon the desirability as well as the feasibility of the development programmes. No study of bureaucracy can, therefore, ignore the bureaucratic interactions with its environment. In a society's environment, the political environment is important because it is the political leaders who determine the systemic goals in a democracy. And since the goal realisation of the system is dependent upon a proper relationship between the political leaders and the bureaucrats, the exploration of certain critical dimensions of their relationship is central to any enquiry about bureaucratic performance. One of these dimensions is the nature and extent of political pressures on the bureaucracy and their consequences for the functioning of bureaucracy as an instrument of development programmes.

The important questions related to the study of political pressure are: How frequently do the politicians exert pressures

26. H.V.R. Iengar, *Administration in India : A Historical Review*, (First ed., Bombay : Bharatiya Vidya Bhavan, 1967), p.41.

upon the bureaucrats ? For what purposes do the politicians bring pressures ? What are the different sources through which the politicians bring pressures ? What consequences do follow for the bureaucrats for not submitting to political pressures ?

Interestingly enough, no bureaucrat in the sample denies the exertion of political pressures, although they differ among themselves in identifying the frequency of political pressures. It is surprising that about seventy percent of the bureaucrats consider political pressures either to be frequent or very frequent.

This study also shows that pressures are brought frequently upon the bureaucrats by politicians for furthering the interests of their friends and relatives. Further, the politicians also pursue the interests of the people of their constituency or locality besides their own interests and those of their family members. By pursuing their own interests and the interests of their family members, politicians in Meghalaya tend to deviate from the universalistic norms.

In bringing pressures upon the bureaucrats, politicians prefer indirect sources to direct sources. While indirect sources of pressures through higher level political leaders, higher level administrators and the administrators' friends and relatives account for 84.73 percent of the responses, the direct sources of pressures like threat consequences, promising better career opportunities and organising demonstrations like gheraos, and dharnas account for 15.27 percent of the responses.

Irrespective of the source or sources used, the exertion of political pressure put the bureaucrats on the horns of a dilemma. If the bureaucrats succumb to political pressure, the legal-rational criteria of bureaucracy are sacrificed and, if they do not, the politicians, who are in a position to take revenge, will be dissatisfied. In such a dilemma, the courses usually resorted to by the bureaucrats are: 'expressing inability due to rules and regulations', 'dealing with the situation themselves but by seeking support either from higher level administrator or higher level political leaders', and 'pushing the matters upwards in the hierarchy'. The other courses of action followed by the bureaucrats are: 'dealing with the situation themselves', and 'seeking transfer to some other place'. Among the courses, 'pushing up the matter' and 'seeking transfer to some other place' are detrimental to the efficient functioning of bureaucracy. While the former results in the congestion of work at the higher level, causing organisational delay and inefficiency, the latter develops an escapist tendency not conducive to healthy bureaucratic functioning.

Further, the study shows that the consequences which follow for not submitting to political pressures such as transfers, spoiling of service records, and non-co-operation and public denigration by political leaders dampen the confidence, initiative and enterprising spirit of the bureaucrats and are detrimental to the development of sound morale and a sense of commitment among them. All these consequences weaken the bureaucracy and do not permit it to act as a vital instrument of socio-economic change.

6

Bureaucratic Dysfunctions

Bureaucratic dysfunction is another important aspect that deserves special attention in study of the problems of bureaucracy. Although Max Weber considered bureaucracy to be superior to all other forms of organisation because of its precision, impersonality and rationality which are conducive to efficient administration,[1] his analysis was of the nature of ideal type bureaucratic functions. He was not concerned with the operational aspects of the ideal-typical characteristics of bureaucracy and thus ignored its dysfunctional aspects.

> In his analysis of bureaucratic structure, Weber focused on official regulations and requirements and their significance for administrative efficiency. Of course, he knew that the behaviour of the members of an organisation does not precisely correspond to its blueprint. But he was not concerned with this problem and did not investigate systematically the way in which operations actually are carried out. Consequently, his analysis ignored the fact that in the course of operations, new elements arise

1. Blau, *op. cit.*, p. 1.

in the structure that influence subsequent operations.[2]

And such elements might be dysfunctional to the bureaucratic organisation.

Although contemporary scholars like Robert Merton have emphasised the dysfunctional aspects of bureaucratic organisation,[3] there are very few scientific, sociological studies of bureaucratic dysfunctions in the Indian context.[4] Referring to corruption as a dysfunctional element in the South Asian countries Gunnar Myrdal points out that it is almost a taboo as a research topic. It is rarely mentioned in scholarly discussion of government and planning revealing a general bias which has been characterised by Prof. Myrdal as "diplomacy in research".[5]

However, bureaucratic dysfunctions in terms of corruption and inefficiency are on the increase in India, and have "become so much a part of everyone's life that people have evolved strategies and styles of operating such a system and the insecurity of dealing with an uncorrupt administration is perhaps what makes people loath to tamper with the existing arrangements".[6] The increasing corruption and inefficiency not only cause loss of time and public money but also affect the stability of the government. If not already, in the near future, it can pose a threat to our democratic system because the post-war history gives ample evidence of the rise of

2. *Ibid.*, p. 2.

3. See Robert K. Merton's "Bureaucratic Structure and Personality" in *Social Theory and Social Structure*, (New-Delhi : Amerind Publishing Co. Pvt. Ltd., 1975), pp. 249-260.

4. One such study has been made by N.K. Singhi in his book *Bureaucracy : Positions and Persons, op. cit.*

5. Gunnar Myrdal, *Asian Drama : An Inquiry into the Poverty of Nations,* Vol. II (London : Allan Lane, The Penguine Press, 1968), pp. 938-939.

6. "Corruption : Third Time Lucky" *Economic and Political Weekly*, Vol. XIII, No. 40 (October 7, 1978), p. 1684.

dictators on the pretext of fighting corruption. As Prof. Myrdal observes :

> The problem is ... of vital concern to the governments in the region [South Asia]. Generally speaking, the habitual practice of bribery and dishonesty tends to pave the way for an authoritarian regime, whose disclosures of corrupt practices in the preceding government and whose punitive action against offenders provide a basis for its initial acceptance by the articulate strata of the population... . The elimination of corrupt practices has also been advanced as the main justification for military take overs. Should the new regime be unsuccessful in its attempts to eradicate corruption, its failure will prepare the ground for a new putsch of some sort. Thus, it is obvious that the extent of corruption has a direct bearing on the stability of South Asian governments.[7]

Bureaucratic dysfunctions in terms of corruption and inefficiency are inter-related and affect not only the day to day life of the citizens but also raise strong obstacles and inhibitions to development. It often promotes irrationality in planning and limits the horizons of plan. The usual way to make money by corrupt practices is to threaten obstruction and delay in official functions and this causes slowing down the wheels of administration in developing countries.[8]

With the above considerations in mind, an attempt is made in the following sections to study the bureaucratic dysfunctions in terms of the corruption and inefficiency. The study will not be an abstract one. Instead, we shall try to answer the questions : What do the bureaucrats think to be the causes of corruption and inefficiency and what remedies do they suggest for removing them from public bureaucracy.

7. Gunnar Myrdal, *op. cit.*, pp. 937-938.
8. *Ibid.*, pp. 951-955.

Corruption

Corruption is an oft-discussed subject in Meghalaya. It pervades all spheres of society in some form or other in varying degrees. Both public discussions and news-paper accounts accord considerable importance to the growing phenomena of political and bureaucratic corruption and inefficiency. The debates in the State Legislation Assembly have quite often dealt with corruption in high places and amongst the bureaucrats and politicians. Stressing the administrative reform as an immediate necessity one Congress M.L.A. Late Shri P.N. Chaudhury thus observed :

> ... Corruption is very rampant in our state [Meghalaya] ; this evil is deep-rooted and unless we can fight against this evil and try to eradicate it from the society we cannot give the real benefits to the people for whom the development programmes are meant to be taken up.[9]

However, corruption in public bureaucracy is not a phenomenon peculiar to Meghalaya, though its ramifications are and pervasive in Meghalaya. Corruption in public bureaucracy is also not something new, but an age old phenomenon. Kautilya in his Arthasastra prescribed measures to be adopted to check corruption. The Mughal period was characterised by bribery, corruption and extortion which led Akbar in 1681 to complain that the clerks and officers of the state have taken to the practice of traders and buy posts with gold and sell them for shameful considerations.[10] During the period of the East India Company, the British Officers and clerks who were virtually the rulers augmented their income through corrupt practices such as collection of graft on taxes

9. *Meghalaya Legislative Assembly Debates*, Vol. IV, No. 4 (Budget Session, 1973), p. 38.

10. G.D. Khosla, "Corruption Down the Ages", *Corruption in India*, ed. Suresh Kohli (First ed., New Delhi : Chetna Publications, 1975), p. 19.

and receipt of gifts.[11] But, soon the Britishers realised that unless they had an honest administration, they would not be able to maintain their political power in India and consequently, they enforced a strict code of integrity. However, the Britishers could not fully eradicate corruption from the public service. There was corruption but till the World War II, corruption was mostly prevalent amongst the lower officials. The higher echelons of bureaucracy were mostly free from this evil. But the immense war efforts during the period of 1939-1945 involved an annual expenditure of hundreds of crores of rupees and the war time controls and scarcities provided ample opportunities for corruption and bribery.[12] This was probably the beginning of mass corruption in India which got its full sway after independence when economic planning and rapid expansion of government activity in new fields involved gigantic public expenditure. There has been a phenomenal increase in corruption in the public services in India since independence. Writing on this subject, G.D. Khosla has pointed out: "...with the realisation of our right in the kind of democracy we had chosen, came the freedom to lie, to cheat, to give and take bribes, to circumvent and to defy the law, to buy positions and power and abuse the power so acquired".[13]

In our attempt to analyse the forms and causes of bureaucratic corruption as perceived by the bureaucrats in Meghalaya, we asked them to identify the important types of corruption prevalent in public bureaucracy in Meghalaya.[14] The question elicited a wide variety of responses which were classified as follows :[15]

11. Bansal, *op. cit.*, p. 2.
12. *Report of the Committee on Prevention of Corruption*, (New-Delhi : Ministry of Home Affairs, Government of India, 1964), pp. 6-7.
13. G.D. Khosla, "Corruption Down the Ages", *Corruption in India*, ed. Suresh Kohli, *op. cit.*, p. 20.
14. For the question, see Appendix C.
15. For analysis of the responses, see Table 6 : 1.

1. Using official position for personal purposes.
2. Using government vehicles for personal work.
3. Bribery.
4. Showing favours to friends and relatives.
5. Using official staff, stationery, etc. for personal work.

We further sought to enquire into the causes of corruption, irrespective of the forms of corruption, as perceived by the bureaucrats by asking them to identify the important causes of corruption.[16] The responses received stand as follows after classification.[17]

1. Moral factor.
2. Economic factor.
3. Political factor.
4. Structural factor.
5. Cultural factor.

Before entering into a discussion of these factors separately, it needs to be said that these factors are inter-related and cannot be studied independently of one another.

Moral factor

Responses like 'no morality', 'no religious faith', 'lack of conscience', etc. are included in the category of 'moral factor' and it is found that 34.78 percent of the responses account for moral weakness and turpitude to be the cause of corruption in public bureaucracy. The factor of moral weakness has been considered from two view points by the respondents :

16. For the question, see Appendix C.

17. For analysis of the responses, see Table 6 : 2.

religious belief and social values. Some of the respondents believe that the morality of the people is becoming weak day-by-day with the advance of modern civilization, and this is because of the fact that people are losing faith in their religions. As one respondent said :

> Lack of religious belief is the main cause of corruption in both our public and private life. Earlier, people had faith in religion and it was the fear of religion which made them abstain from doing immoral things. Today, religious hold is becoming loose day-by-day. No longer people think about the day of judgement and they value the persent more than the future.

Another cause of moral weakness is the replacement of social values, like 'service', 'sufferings' and 'sacrifice' by the new acquisitive values. New acquisitive values are in turn the result of a complex combination of factors. People's aspirations were raised during the nationalist movement by promising them a high standard of living. After independence, the programme of economic development and modernisation promised eradication of poverty and increase of national income. Though goals were proclaimed, the means to realise the goals were lacking. This imbalance between goals and means resulted in the adoption of extra-legal means. Besides, the model of modernisation envisaged by planners is based on the affluent and advanced societies of the West. To follow this model, the norms and values of traditional society have been undermined, and the society has come to acquire a new set of norms and values. Status in the modern society is judged through economic success rather than traditional indices. People have developed increased desire for consumption of newer articles which not only provide comfort but are also considered to be a status symbol. And this desire for consumption can be met only through acquiring wealth. "Wealth, however, acquired is an effective passport to honour, power and influence".[18]

18. Quoted by John B. Monteiro, *Corruption : Control of Maladministration*, (First ed., Bombay : Manaktalas, 1966), p. 64

The bureaucrat being a part of the society cannot be expected to develop values different from those of society. They are in constant interaction with the society, and as a result of this interaction they influence and, in turn, are influenced by the society. "The standards of people influence those of public officials and it is hard to develop honest officials in a corrupt society. But it is equally true that high standard on the part of officials and public leaders raise the level of the whole community".[19] The bureaucrats, being the executors of various development programmes, have more opportunities to misuse their power and indulge in the acts of corruption more than others. In an acquisitive society, where people are judged by what they have rather than what they are, bureaucrats cannot be expected to develop personal virtues or a sense of morality. This lack of a sense of morality has led to a scramble for the acquisition of material gains and prizes irrespective of the means adopted.

Economic factor

Next to moral factor is the economic factor which accounts for 30.43 percent of the responses. In this category of economic factor we included responses like 'poor salary', 'family burden', 'greediness', etc. Respondents who were interviewed were found to be vocal about the gap between the cost of living and the salary they received, although, in the same breath, they pointed out that sheer poverty was not always responsible for corruption. According to most of the respondents, poverty, along with lack of honesty and integrity, causes corruption. Thus, it is neither the economic factor nor the moral factor alone, but a combination of the two that causes corruption. This aspect is well reflected in the following comment of a respondent :

> Presume for example that I am a corrupt officer. I take bribes. I use my official position for non-official purposes. But why do I do all these things ? I am an officer having

19. *Ibid.*, p. 67.

a family of five members. I have a status not only in my office but also in the society. Corresponding to this status, some social roles are assigned to me. I must have a servant, I must attend parties and other such social get-togethers (both official and non-official). When I go out for marketing or on a social courtesy visit, I should not walk, and even if I do, my wife must not walk because an officer's wife is more or less a 'maharani'. My wife must be well-dressed when she goes out, otherwise, salesmen at the counter will address her 'Didi' instead of 'Madam' and her host will not see her off at the road-side. Besides, I have social obligations and the responsibility to educate my children. But wherefrom I will do all these things ? From my salary ! It is too little an amount. So, I have two alternatives open to me. Either I shall be a role-deviant (but in this case there is every possibility of disturbing family peace) or I must adopt some extra legal means. This is not something unique in my case, but common to most of the officers. In such a dilemma, either of the two alternatives is to be followed, and mostly the second, because it promises a happy life and probably a bright future.

Another aspect of this economic factor as emphasized by some respondents is the greediness for acquiring more and more money and other material benefits. Although this is a common human desire, in some cases, it is insatiable and leads to increasing illegal gratification of the same.

Political factor

Responses like 'political interference', 'favours shown under political pressure', 'illegal things done under political direction', etc., are grouped under political factor which accounts for 20.87 percent of the responses. The respondents have not pointed out cases of bribery among the politicians. Cases most frequently mentioned by them relate to illegal gratification of the demands of the relatives of politicians. Illegal gratification can be of various types and forms. Ranging from providing several fringe benefits, it may include granting of an industrial licence, export-import licence or issuing contracts to the family members, relatives, friends and favourities of the politicians in power. Once, the researcher was present when an officer was instructing the son of the ex-Chief Minister how to apply for a contract and what would be the charge to be shown in the tender. Such favours are shown under unwritten instructions of political bosses which influence the decisions of the bureaucrats while issuing licences, permits, and contracts. The ruling party must oblige those who give donations to their election funds which cannot be done without the help of the bureaucrats. The President of a State Chamber of Commerce once said : "Political leaders pressurised the trades and industry to make unlimited donations ...which resulted in price rise. ... These are realised on grounds of licencing, quota and permits, not out of affection, but to protect trade and industry".[20] If a bureaucrat acts at the behest of the politicians, he is rewarded, and if he sticks to principles, rules and procedures and refuses their requests, he is subjected to harassment. The bureaucrats who act in order to please the politicians, thus, violate the bureaucratic norms of impartiality and neutrality.

Structural factor

In the category of 'structural factor', responses like 'delay', 'redtapism', 'complicated rules and regulations', etc., are included and these account for 12.61 percent of the responses. The bureaucratic system in India continued the complex set of rules established by the colonial rulers as a means of maintaining control over their Indian subordinates with various levels of training, outlook and goals. The diversity and complexity of these rules have led to an 'administrative jungle'. In Meghalaya, separate set of rules for the tribal areas framed by the different District Councils have further added to this complexity. This complexity of rules and regulations, sometimes,

20. Quoted by Dev Dutt, "In Politics", *Corruption in India*, ed., Suresh Kohli, *op.cit.*, p. 94.

becomes a source of corruption. The bureaucrats, sometimes, deliberately make delay in their decisions so as to receive bribes and other pecuniary benefits. The clients, on the other hand, offer bribes to the bureaucrats in order to be free from or circumvent the bureaucratic web of cumbersome and complex rules and procedures.[21] Besides, most of the people do not know much about the governmental rules and procedures and find it necessary to take recourse to the unwritten but more effective ways of getting things done by governmental agencies.

Cultural factor

Under cultural factor we included responses like 'habit' and 'familial tradition' which account for only 1.30 percent of the responses. Although negligible from the numerical point of view, such responses indicate that corruption can be habitual and such a habit can be influenced by the familial background of the bureaucrats. As one bureaucrat commented :

> There are two types of corrupt persons not only in the bureaucracy but also in society. Some people are corrupt by nature or habit, others are made corrupt by their poor economic conditions or by the environment in which they work. Persons in the first category are not born with corrupt habits but familial traditions make them corrupt. In most of such cases, you will find either the parents or other members of the family earning through dishonest means and this behaviour of the elders influences the young who start considering such a thing as a natural way of living. And, if such a person enters the government service, he cannot give up his habit which is formed during the early years of his life.

Measures against Corruption

Having analysed the causes of corruption, we will now

21. Singhi, *op. cit.*, p. 202.

discuss the measures for the removal of corruption from the bureaucracy, a problem which is of great concern to both the public and the government. For this purpose, we asked the bureaucrats to suggest some important remedial measures for removing corruption from the public services.[22] In response to this, a wide variety of suggestions were provided which we categorised into four : Social, Economic, Political and Structural.[23]

Social values

Surprisingly, almost half of the responses (48.15 percent) account for a change in societal value-structure as a remedy of corruption in public bureaucracy. This emphasis upon social values is due to the fact that bureaucracy being a subsystem of the social system cannot undergo basic changes without bringing about changes in the value structure of the society. Further, the lack of morality, as highlighted to be a cause of corruption, is relative and depends upon societal values. Not only morality, but also economic, political and cultural factors are influenced by the value structure of society. Nearly 50.00 percent of respondents, therefore, lay emphasis upon a basic change in social values as a remedial measure for removing corruption from public bureaucracy. A bureaucrat commented thus :

No such measure like vigilance commission[24] or enact-

22. For the question, see Appendix C.
23. For analysis of the responses, see Table 6:3.
24. In this connection, it may be pointed out that though there is an anticorruption wing of the CID under the Deputy Inspector General of Police in Meghalaya, its functionings are beset with certain difficulties. In the words of the Chief Minister "...the work of the branch is too difficult because we do not have trained personnel with sufficient experience in this specialised work ... Our difficulty is that specific instances are not coming forward, and we do not get witness to substantiate the allegations". See *Meghalaya Legislative Assembly Debates*, Vol. X, No. 2, (Budget Session, 1975), p. 83.

ment of stringent laws will be an adequate answer to the menace of corruption. Though law cannot be made fool-proof but even if it can be, its implementation depends upon man who is a social animal and who, in due course of time, will become corrupt. Income-tax, Sales-tax, Police, Customs and Central Excise-such half-a-dozen examples can be readily given. If the evil is to be eliminated, we must go to the root of it, and that root lies in society. Today, the society has lost its values. Honesty and integrity no longer count much. A man is judged by what he has—rather than by what he is. There was a time when society looked down upon its dishonest and corrupt members. But today it is not the case. When parents arrange the marriage of their daughter, they consider the material possessions of the bride-groom more than his honesty and integrity. So, what can a youngman do ? Instead of being rewarded, a honest person is punished by the society. Until and unless our social values are changed and society itself wages a war against its corrupt members, we cannot hope to eliminate corruption from the bureaucracy.

Social value system is undoubtedly an important factor in the establishment of a clean and efficient administrative system. Its importance has also been emphasised by the Chief Minister W. A. Sangma when he said :

> ...unless and until there is a change of character in our society is it possible to talk about a clean and efficient administration ? I would very much like to have it and I am sure everyone would like to have it, but where lies the responsibility ? The responsibility lies with you and me, with the masses of the people in the State...it is a fact that if one wants to get more than what is due to him it means corruption and exploitation. Is it possible for the government alone to rectify this ? ...this problem concerns the entire society. Unless the society itself wants to have a clean and efficient administration it will not be possible to bring about that type of administration simply by trying

to remove certain officers from government machinery.[25]

Economic measures

Economic measure accounts for 27.28 percent of the responses. Responses like, 'more salary', 'more monetary benefits', etc., are included in this category. It believed that if bureaucrats are well paid or paid proportionately to the cost of living, the rate of malpractices will diminish. Earlier, while pointing out the economic strain upon the bureaucrats, a reference was made to the gross disparities of pay-scales and other monetary benefits between the State Government employees and the Central Government empoyees as well as between the higher and lower officials. During our discussion we raised the questions : Is it justified to pay more to the Central Government employees than their State counterparts when they live in the same town or same area and perform the same functions ? Such disparities cause a feeling of deprivation in the minds of the State Government employees, and consequently, lead to the adoption of unfair means by them to compensate for their inadequate salaries. According to some of our respondents, this malady can be remedied by raising the salary of the State Government employees at par with the Central Government employees as it has already been done in the case of some states.

It is to be observed here that an increase in the salaries of the State Government employees alone will not solve the problem. There are no equal economic opportunities in India. Economic power has been concentrated in the hands of a few, and this has led to an alliance among industrialists-capitalists, politicians and bureaucrats. Further, concentration of economic power in the hands of a few gives them control over vantage positions in the government and even on policy making. Unless a reasonable degree of economic equality is established, a more reduction of disparities in salary scales

25. *Meghalaya Legislative Assembly Debates,* Vol. 1, No. 1, (April Session, 1970), pp. 58-59.

will not remove corruption from the bureaucracy.

Political factors

Political factor includes responses like stopping 'political interference' and 'political pressure' and accounts for 12.50 percent of the responses. It is said that if political interference in the day-to-day administration ceases, there would be a decrease in corruption and malpractices.

Related to this is the wider question of the nature of political leadership and the values and standards adopted by ministers and other political leaders. It is of utmost importance that the leaders set an example by refraining from indulging in acts of corruption and favouritism. The basic cause of corruption in the bureaucracy lies in the political sphere-corruption at the highest level in government and political parties. This, however, involves problems which are beyond the scope of the present enquiry.

Structural Reforms

Structural reform includes responses like 'avoidance of delay', 'introduction of simple rules and regulations', etc., which account for 11.57 percent of the responses. It is suggested that instead of lengthy and cumbersome procedures, simple procedures should be introduced in order to avoid delay which is one of the basic causes of corruption in public bureaucracy. Complex procedures and detailed and lengthy rules not only cause delay but also result in dampening individual initiative and ability.[26] Time limits should be prescribed for dealing with receipts, files and the performance of other duties and these should be strictly enforced. Superior officers should consider it their responsibility to find out whether in any particular matter

26. K.N. Butani "Leadership in Administration", *The Indian Journal of Public Administration*, Vol. II, No. 4 (October-December, 1956), pp. 325-326.

there has been avoidable delay and call to account the person responsible for delay.

On the subject of cumbersome, complex and unimaginative procedures in administration, Dr. Paul H. Appleby made the following observation which need special attention :

> The rules of business, Secretariat Instructions and Office Manuals seems to me to be generally too didactic and confusing, too detailed and unimaginative. They might be expected to contribute to the extreme insistence on following formal channels too literally and invariably. They seem to assume and encourage that literal mindedness which damps the spirit, imagination and judgement which are important to good administration.[27]

Inefficiency

Inefficiency is another aspect of bureaucratic dysfunction in India. The study of the perception of inefficiency is important because it affects the goal achievement of the system. It is also responsible for making the administration unpopular, and in turn, the government, because the people judge the governmental performance through the effectiveness of its administrative machinery. The complexities of a modern democratic government demand, more than before, an efficient administrative machinery and competent and capable administrators to operate that machinery. However, according to many observers and critics, growing corruption and inefficiency are the most notorious and distinguishing features of Indian administration. As Prof. Rajni Kothari has observed "...if there is any arm of the Indian polity that is ridden with confusion, indeterminacy and inertia, it is the administration. Nothing is more urgent than infusing change and dynamics to this arm of government. But nothing is more neglected and more resistant to change".[28]

27. Appleby, *op.cit.*, p. 14.
28. Rajni Kothari, "Foreword" *Administrative Change in India*, ed. Ramesh K. Aurora, *op.cit.*, p. 111.

One of the important questions relating to inefficiency in Indian administration is : what are the causes of bureaucratic inefficiency and how can it be removed ? For studying the causes of bureaucratic inefficiency, we asked the respondents to specify some important causes of inefficiency.[29] The question elicited different responses which were classified into the following categories :[30]

1. Administrative.
2. Political.
3. Social.
4. Individual.
5. Economic.

Administrative Causes

24.25 percent of the respondents were found to consider bureaucratic inefficiency as resulting from administrative causes like 'complicated procedures', 'lack of co-ordination', 'red-tape' etc. Procedures, instead of serving as a means to an end, sometimes become an end in themselves. Robert Merton has drawn attention to this tendency in the following words : "Adherence to the rules, originally conceived as a means, become transformed into an end-in-itself ; there occurs the familiar process of displacement of goals whereby an instrumental value becomes a terminal value".[31]

Almost everyday, some or other new rules, regulations and procedures are introduced which result in the creation of a jungle of procedures. These procedures are 'archaic, unimaginative, anachronistic, and cumbersome' and lead to red-

29. For the question, see Appendix C.
30. For analysis of the responses, see Table 6:4.
31. Merton, *op.cit.*, p. 253.

tapism and delay in making decisions, in the movement of files and accomplishment of other work. A matter of minor importance passes through half-a-dozen hands ; thus, making almost everyone busy for nothing. This aspect of cumbersome rules and regulations has been graphically illustrated by L.K. Jha. He writes :

> If someone asks me a question, the first thing I ask myself is whether it is within my competence to give him a reply, this is never easy for anyone to know. So, I start consulting everybody else who might possibly be concerned or interested. Before they give me any answer, they ask me a number of questions. I fling them back at the chap who approached me first. If he still persevers and comes back with answers, I pass them back to my colleagues. If they can find no flaw in the answers, they take a decision. And usually, the decision is to put the matter up to the officers above them. And so the game goes on. Do you think I like it ? When I retire, the very rules and procedures which I apply will result in my pension being held up for months and even years. And when it is sanctioned, I shall have to prove by producing certificates on the prescribed forms that I am alive and also that I was alive in each of the intervening months during which my pension was under consideration ; yet what am I to do ? People think I exercise authority. They do not know that I have no authority. Where the authority lies, no one knows. All I know is that if I do nothing, no one will blame me, but if I do something, then many people will ask me whether what I did was correct. Correct, mind you, not right. If I help someone, my motives may be questioned. If I say no, I am safe. So, I take the line of least assistance.[32]

Not only cumbersome procedures, but also the lack of co-ordination causes inefficiency. Modern welfare administration

32. L.K. Jha, "Mr Red Tape", *The Indian Journal of Public Administration*, Vol. XI, No. 4 (October-December, 1965), pp. 681-682.

requires co-ordination between different departments, and hierarchies and between different units or branches of the same department. But in Meghalaya, there is no rational system followed in co-ordinating the work of different ministries and departments, and consequently, there is delay and inefficiency in the administration.

Political Causes

Responses like 'political interference', 'political pressures', 'political victimization', etc., are included in political causes which account for 21.64 percent of the total responses. Politicians often interfere in administration and bring pressure upon the administrators to get things done according to their whims and interests. Faced with such pressures, the administrators take recourse to the game of 'passing the buck' or take shelter under the sanctuary or rules and regulations. Victimization of the bureaucrats on political grounds dampens their initiative and morale. There develops a tendency towards 'playing safe' and one of the most commonly-adopted ways of 'playing safe' is to follow the precedents. Though the observance of precedents in making decisions is an element of bureaucratic rationality,[33] sometimes regard for precedents verges on morbidity. Precedents, thus, are no longer treated as one of the ingredients in a rational decision but degenerate into a means for avoiding fresh thinking and quick decisions. "Routine, red-tape, and long-noting take the place of initiative, ingenuity and innovation".[34]

Social Causes

Social causes like 'groupism', 'communalism', etc., are also considered to be responsible for bureaucratic inefficiency

33. R.P. Khosla, "Bureaucrats : The Loss of Vision", *The Indian Journal of Public Administration*, Vol. XI, No. 1, (January-March, 1965), pp. 36-39.
34. N.V. Gadgil, "Accountability of Admintstration", *The Indian Journal of Public Administration*, Vol. 1, No. 3, (July-September, 1955), p. 195.

which account for 20.90 percent of the responses in this study. As we discussed earlier, the Meghalayan Society as well as the administration is divided into two hostile camps of 'insiders' and 'outsiders' (the 'tribals' and 'non-tribals') on the basis of region and community. This 'insiders'-'outsiders' relationship sometimes takes the form of cliques leading to mutual hostility and mistrust, thereby, adversely affecting bureaucratic performance and efficiency.

Individual factor

Individual factors like 'lack of initiative', 'devotion to one's duties', 'punctuality', etc., are also considered to be a factor responsible for administrative inefficiency and account for 18.66 percent of the total responses. Initiative and interest are personal traits and depend upon the complex interaction of different factors like family up-bringing, the influence of social and educational institutions and bureaucratic culture.

Included in the individual factor are such traits as 'devotion to one's duties', 'ability to perform one's task', 'punctuality' and 'diligence'. These traits, however, have to be assessed at the stage of recruitment. With a policy of large-scale reservations in government service (85 percent), it cannot be said that the best talents (possessing the qualities of devotion, diligence, etc.) are recruited in the public services of Meghalaya.

Economic factor

'Bribery' and 'monetary benefits' are included in the category of economic factor which accounts for 14.55 percent of the responses. And here we come across the interaction between corruption and inefficiency—the two inter-related aspects of bureaucratic dysfunction. Corrupt practices result in delay, and in turn, it is delay that causes corruption. A corrupt official deliberately makes delay in taking decisions or disposing of a matter, so that he can earn something by way of grease money. Very often, a bribe-giver does not wish to get anything done unlawfully, but just wants to speed up the movement of files and communication from department to department or from branch to branch of the same department. In certain offices, especially the executive offices, every movement of files is facilitated by 'speed money'. Unless and until 'speed money' is paid, the official will not be found in his seat, and even if he is found, he will not give any attention to the client or will be unable to locate the relevant papers.[35] Sometimes, even the bearer needs to be paid for locating the file in the chamber of the officer. The amount of speed money varies from case to case and from person to person. This has become such a matter of routine that a complaint becomes totally infructuous, its only effect being that it may invite harassment to the complainant. Besides being one of the most unhealthy corrupt practices, it clogs the wheels of bureaucratic machinery and is one of the most important causes of delay and inefficiency.

Remedial Measures against Inefficiency

After discussing the causes of inefficiency, the corollary question is : what measures are necessary for making bureaucracy efficient ? It is not easy to answer this question. However, we asked the respondents to name important remedial measures to be adopted for removing inefficiency from the public bureaucracy.[36] The responses received were categorised into three :[37]

35. This aspect of bureaucratic inefficiency has been highlighted in the floor of the Assembly. Making charges against the Deputy Commissioner's office and the Treasury office in Shillong one M.L.A. observed ..."I should say that it is a tragedy. It is an everyday happening that the bill do not move unless some money passes. A person who goes there for the bill will have to push a 5 or 10 rupee note and if this is not done, the bill will not move and he will have to go away. He is promised to pass the bill next-day but then his bills are just blocked there. A person who has to get his bills passed in the Treasury has to undergo unimaginable troubles and misery...", See *Meghalaya Legislative Assembly Debates*, Vol. I, No. 1, (March-April Session, 1972), p. 89.

36. For the question, see Appendix C.

37. For analysis of the responses, see Table 6:5.

1. Administrative.
2. Political.
3. Individual.

The responses show that none of the respondents suggested social and economic measures as a remedy for bureaucratic inefficiency, although some of them considered social and economic factors to be responsible for bureaucratic inefficiency. They did not suggest social measures probably because they considered society an independent variable. The reason for not suggesting economic measures is probably for the close affinity between corruption and inefficiency. They perhaps thought that if one was eliminated, the other would cease to exist.

Administrative Measures

Under administrative measure, we included responses like 'simplification of rules and regulations', 'proper co-ordination', 'proper personnel planning', etc., which accounts for 36.50 percent of the responses. This emphasis upon administrative measures is because of the fact that it is the immediate sphere with which they are concerned and that much can be done in the administrative sphere for improving its efficiency. This aspect has been discussed at some length in the preceding pages.

Political Measures

Political measures account for 33.08 percent of the responses and include responses like 'non-interference by the politicians', 'code of conduct for politicians', 'demarcation of political and administrative functions', etc. As we have already discussed, it is believed that there would be efficiency in the administration if politicians behave responsibly and do not interfere in the day-to-day working of the administration. Further, it has also been pointed out that if bureaucracy is to function efficiently, bureaucrats should not be made scapegoats. As one respondent commented :

> Half of the bureaucratic inefficiency would be eliminated our politicians are trained in a training school in the art of behaving with the administrators in a parliamentary democracy.

Measures for improving Individual Standard and Ability

Measures in this category account for 30.41 percent of the responses. In this category, respondents emphasised the importance of recruitment of suitable candidates which depends upon the recruitment policy of the government. It was suggested that recruitment policy should be made objective and scientific,[38] so that, only the best candidates would be recruited. Besides, the need for training has also been emphasised. Recruitment of the best talents by itself is not an effective guarantee for increasing efficiency in the administration. Talented candidates must have proper and thorough training in the art of administration. In this connection, it may be pointed out that, excepting the Police Training School for subordinate police officials, there is no provision for training Civil Servants in Meghalaya.

Summary

Dysfunction is an important aspect in the study of bureau-

38. Although the bureaucrats, irrespective of their community, emphasised the need for effective recruitment policy, there were differences in their views over the question of reservation. The tribal officers are in favour of continuing the reservation policy while the non-tribals are opposed to it. The non-tribal officers hold that if 85 percent of the jobs in government offices are kept reserved, the best talent cannot be inducted in public service, and consequently, administrative efficiency will suffer. The tribal officers, on the other hand, defend the reservation policy on the ground that when about 80 percent of the people in the state belong to Scheduled Tribes and Scheduled Castes, 85 percent reservation for this category is not unreasonable.

cracy, which manifests especially in the bureaucracies of developing societies. Corruption and inefficiency are the two important manifestations of bureaucratic dysfunction. There is cause and effect relationship between corruption and inefficiency, and hence, none of these can be studied in complete isolation of the other.

The bureaucratic perception of corruption includes bribery, using official position for non-official purposes, using official staff, stationery and vehicles for personal use, and showing favours to relations and friends, all of which are opposed to the norms of Weber's ideal rational bureaucracy.

The bureaucrats consider moral, economic, political, structural and cultural factors as being responsible for corruption in public bureaucracy. Among the remedial measures to eradicate corruption, they suggest societal, economic, political and structural measures. The absence of any remedial of any measures in the shape of individual morality is perhaps is due to the fact that morality is dependent upon the value structure of society and it is because of this fact that societal measures have been emphasized by the bureaucrats.

The other aspect of bureaucratic dysfunction, namely, inefficiency, is a major obstacle in implementing various programmes of development. In the present study, it is found that the respondents consider administrative, political, social, individual and economic factors responsible for bureaucratic inefficiency ; and for removing inefficiency, they suggest administrative, political and individual measures. The respondents do not suggest social and economic measures for removing inefficiency, though they consider social and economic factors responsible for bureaucratic inefficiency. The absence of social measures can be attributed to the fact that they consider society an independent variable, while the absence of economic measure can be accounted for by the close affinity between corruption and inefficiency.

7

Conclusion

The higher bureaucracy plays an important role in the formulation and implementation of governmental policy both in the developed and developing nations. With the assumption of new tasks and activities in the sphere of development and welfare, governmental functions have multiplied, underscoring the role and importance of bureaucracy. This is more so in a developing country like India which is committed to the goal of rapid socio-economic development. The Preamble of the Indian Constitution proclaims liberty, equality, secularism, socialism and democracy as the objectives of the state. The Preamble guarantees social, economic and political justice; liberty of thought, expression, belief, faith and worship; and equality of status and opportunity for all members of society. This implies that India is to follow the ideals of Welfare State where there would be equality of status and opportunity for all its citizens.

The Directive Principles of State Policy further enjoin upon the State the responsibility to promote the welfare of the people by securing and protecting a social order in which social, economic and political justice shall inform all institutions of national life. The Directive Principles visualize an economic and social order based on equality of opportunity, full employment, provision of adequate means of livelihood and social security benefits for all its citizens.

The realisation of all these ideals and objectives call for a rapid development in social, economic and political spheres. For achieving rapid social and economic development, it is the government which has to initiate, plan, undertake and execute development programmes. The state and government thus become the principal instrument of change. Prof. Joseph LaPalombara brings this out succintly in the following words :

> It scarcely requires exhaustive documentation to demonstrate that major changes in both the developed and the developing nations are inconceivable today without the massive intervention of government. The time is evidently past when public officials are expected to sit on the developmental sidelines, limiting their roles of the fixing of general rules and to providing certain basic services and incentives for those private entrepreneurs who are major players in the complicated and exciting game of fashioning profound changes in economic and social systems. Whether it is the encouragement of electronic industries in the industrialised West, or the improvement of rice production in Pakistan or Vietnam, or an increase in medical care in the United States, or the exploitation of petroleum resources in Latin America or the Middle East, the direct participation of government is immediate and intimate, if not to say exclusive. When our focus shifts from the economic to other areas of activity, the presence of government is revealed in even sharper relief. Systematic campaigns to eradicate illiteracy, create or revitalize village-level government, remove ancient social barriers, or to replace atomistic parochialism with a sense of nationhood are unthinkable without the participation of government. The same may be said for any effort to forge major transformations in the political institutions that characterize any

particular society.[1]

The public bureaucracy is the only instrument of action available to governments for realising their programmes of socio-economic change because "... the bureaucracy husbands the vast majority of whatever necessary professional, technical and entrepreneurial resources may be available to a society committed to change".[2]

But, what role does the higher bureaucracy in Meghalaya play in the socio-economic transformation of the state? Critics of Indian bureaucracy (of which the Meghalayan bureaucracy is a part) are of the view that there exists a dichotomy between bureaucratic disposition and the needs of development. Writing about the role of bureaucracy in economic development, Prof. S.C. Dube pointed out :

> Its structure and ethos suited it more for maintenance of law and order than for massive nation-building : its adaptation to the emerging milieu has been beset with organisational incompatibilities, psychological resistances and value conflicts. In consequence, it suffers from certain lags and finds itself unable to grapple with the new challenges with ease and confidence. There doubtless is some evidence of adaptation, adjustment, and accommodation, but on the whole the situation is still largely fluid.[3]

Similarly, Joseph LaPalombara advances the view that in the context of political and economic development :

> ... public administrators steeped in the tradition of Indian

1. Joseph LaPalombara, "An Overview", *Bureaucracy and Political Development,* ed. Joseph LaPalombara (Princeton, New Jersey : Princeton University Press, 1967), pp. 4-5.
2. *Ibid.*, p. 5.
3. S.C. Cube, "Bureaucracy and Economic Development", *The Indian Journal of Public Administration,* Vol. XII, No. 3, (July-September, 1966), p. 384.

> Civil Service may be lese useful as developmental entrepreneurs than those who are not so rigidly tied to notions of bureaucratic status, hierarchy and impartiality. The economic development of a society, particularly if it is to be implemented by massive intervention of the public sector, requires a breed of bureaucrats different (e.g., more free-wheeling, less adhering to administrative forms, less attached to the importance of hierarchy and seniority) from the type of man who is useful when the primary concern of bureaucracy is the maintenance of law and order.[4]

The above general evaluation of Indian bureaucracy by social scientists stresses the point that the existing values and attitudes of the Indian bureaucrats are not suited to the tasks and demands of nation-building and socio-economic development and that the main cause of this is the colonial administrative legacy and failure of political leadership to develop the needed orientations among the bureaucrats in keeping with the new tasks and challenges.

For understanding the role of bureaucracy in development due attention needs to be given to the bureaucratic organisational structure as well as to the bureaucratic behaviour because developmental administration refers to the organisational structure, and values and attitudes which are necessary for the implementation of schemes and programmes of socio-economic and political change undertaken by the government.[5] Thus, here, the study will be divided into two parts : in the first part, we shall deal with the organisational structure of bureaucracy in Meghalaya while, in the second part, we shall deal with the values and attitudes of the bureaucrats in Meghalaya towards developmental goals.

4. Joseph LaPalombara, "An Overview", *Bureaucracy and Political Development*, ed. Joseph LaPalombara, *op. cit.*, p. 12.
5. V.A. Pai Panandiker, "Developmental Administration : An Approach", *The Indian Journal of Public Administration*, Vol. X, No. 1, (January- March, 1964), pp. 35-36.

A study of the role of bureaucratic organisational structure in the development of the state gives rise to the following questions : who are the bureaucrats and how are they organised ? What was the motivation of the bureaucrats in joining public services ? Are they satisfied with their jobs ? What is the relations of the bureaucrats amongst themselves as well as with their political masters ? How far are they honest and efficient ? Although these questions cannot be claimed to be exhaustive, they are some of the basic questions related to the goal-achievement of the system having an important bearing on the role of bureaucracy in development. We examine these questions in the following section in the light of our findings in the preceding chapters.

In answering the question—who are the bureaucrats ?, as our study of the social and economic composition of the bureaucrats in an earlier chapter has shown, we may generalise that a great majority of the bureaucrats in the sample were from the urbanised middle-class families. 76.36 percent of the bureaucrats in our sample have had an urban background while 85.46 percent of the people in the state live in rural areas. Again, 60.89 percent of the bureaucrats have had an annual parental income of Rs. 5,000/- and above. This urban middle-class orientation of the higher bureaucrats poses a dilemma ; being predominantly a rural state, Meghalaya has emphasised rural programme in its developmental plan.[6] Although the correlation between the socio-economic background of the bureaucrats and the nature of their functioning yet remains to be established, Richard Taub in his study of Bhubaneswar has noted the ignorance of the urbanised bureaucrats about the problems of rural India.[7] While speaking in a Conference (Morale in the Public Service, organised by the IIPA), one participant raised a question in regard to the attitudes of the public servant to the work that he does and observed :

6. For details about the state's plan, see *Draft Annual Plan, 1978-79*, Planning Department, Government of Meghalaya.

7. Taub, *op.cit.*, pp. 122-125.

> ... I have a feeling that public services in our country are manned primarily by the urban sections of the population, while the plan we are trying to put through and the series of which will follow, are directed primarily to making an impact on the rural life of the community. I do not khow whether the kind of faith we would like to see in the public services would [be] generated among the people who are not really so much at one with the interests of the bulk of the population. It is true, of course, that as education advances there will be greater and greater degree of urbanisation and since in the public services you get educated sections, they have to be perhaps, more urban in their ideal and outlook than the rest of the countrymen. But I always feel that there is the sort of an initial hiatus between the public services and the major section of the population. I do not know how this gap could be reduced, whether the methods of recruitment could be suitably altered in order to see that there is not much emphasis on urbanisation, so that there is greater realisation of the needs of the rural population among the services.[8]

The other structural elements of the organisation in Meghalaya are also not suitable for effective bureaucratic performance. As at the centre and in other states, in Meghalaya also there exists parallel services, each with its own service conditions, giving birth to jealousies and animosities and a feeling of class and status consciousness among the bureaucrats. The class and status consciousness are a barrier to co-operative functioning among the bureaucrats, and thus, anti-developmental. A thinly veiled authoritarian hierarchy with an elite class of service to boss over other services has caused low morale and frustration amongst public servants. Besides, the positions at the upper level of the hierarchy are very few and far between and this results in the congestion

8. C.D. Deshmukh, Chairman, *Morale in the Public Service* (Report of a Conference, January 3-4, 1959), (New-Delhi : Indian Institute of Public Administration, August, 1959), p. 17.

of work at the upper level causing unmanageability and delay. The outmoded rules, regulations and procedures of the colonial period instead of being revamped are continued only to cause exasperating delay in developmental and administrative work, dilution of responsibility almost to the point of irresponsibility and morbid preoccupation with rules, regulations and precedents, rather than the achievement of programmatic objectives and performance of tasks. Further, cumbersome and complex procedures result in cross-references between a number of departments without any co-ordinating machinery. And the lack of co-ordination between different departments acts as a deterrent to the realisation of planned objectives. Commenting on the non-utilisation of monetary grant by some departments, the Public Accounts Committee in its report for the year 1972-73 regretted "... to note that due to lack of co-ordination... huge amounts of both plan and non-plan [money] were surrendered and the objectives of budgeting were not achieved".[9]

The intrusion of communal and familial factors also need to be noted in a study of the organisation of public bureaucracy in Meghalaya. Although the classification is not exhaustive, the bureaucracy in Meghalaya is divided into two camps i.e., 'insiders' and 'outsiders' which retards the team work and co-operative functioning of the bureaucrats. Even if such considerations did not in fact influence decisions, the suspicion that they do, proves more harmful than what is done by actual decisions. Every promotion or transfer, however, justly done or based on impersonal ground is deemed capricious and based on clique animosities. There are tensions and suspicion between the 'insiders' and 'outsiders' which sometimes come into the open and give rise to a feeling of vindictiveness. As a protection against individual helplessness in the face of such vindictiveness, the individual depends on his faction and factional alliances. But the existence of factions among the bureaucrats is detrimental to

9. *Public Accounts Committee Report*, 1972-73, Meghalaya Legislative Assembly, p. 24, para, 30.1.

effective bureaucratic performance as it diverts their energy from performance of tasks to factional or group politics. Writing about particularistic orientations as obstacles to economic development in underdeveloped countries, Hoselitz aptly observes :

> The demands of economic development in all these countries [developing countries] require the elimination or effective reduction of particularist loyalties and action based upon them. For if the human and non-human resources of a country are to be allocated optimally, strict principles of efficiency, rather than familiarity or other forms of personal and local preference, must rule in the assignment of economic and occupational roles and similar contractual relations pertaining to allocation of resources. But local, tribal, and linguistic particularisms stand in the way of this process of generalisation of interpersonal economic relations in a developing country and hence the pressures for economic development tend to support the struggle against them.[10]

Another factor which impedes effective role-performance by the bureaucracy in Meghalaya is the compartmentalisation of bureaucrats into the 'generalists' and the 'specialists' and the 'I.A.S.' and the 'non-I.A.S.' As already pointed out in a preceding chapter, the generalist domination of the administration is resented by the specialists in Meghalaya. It is considered to be inimical to the tasks of modernisation and development. In this connection, Prof. LaPalombara rightly observes :

> It seems clear that one serious impediment to economic development in the newer states is the domination of public administration by the administrative generalist. In so far as developmental goals imply highly specialised

10. B.F. Hoselitz, "Levels of Economic Performance and Bureaucratic Structure", *Bureaucracy and Political Development*, ed. Joseph LaPalombara, *op. cit.*, p. 191.

administrative roles—in either the public or the private sector—the persistence of administrative generalists will constitute an impediment to economic change.[11]

Further, the division of bureaucrats into the 'I.A.S.' and the 'non-I.A.S.' groups gives rise to a feeling of mutual hatred and jealousy which hinder co-operation among the bureaucrats, and thus, prevent them from functioning as a team for the realisation of systemic goals.

Another problem the higher bureaucracy faces in Meghalaya is the wide-spread dissatisfaction of its members with different aspects of the job. The prevalence of such wide-spread dissatisfaction and frustration among the Civil Servants in Meghalaya is a major impediment to the realisation of development goals because, as Prof. V.A. Pai Panandiker says "...motivation and job-satisfaction of the Civil Servants are the most crucial factors that impinge directly on their efficiency, morale and further development; that no amount of institutional sophistication would be as important to the administrative performance of the governmental machinery as motivation and job satisfaction of its personnel".[12]

The administrative scene also witnesses increasing violations of bureaucratic organisational norms such as those relating to security, tenure of posts, assignments, transfers and promotions. The bureaucracy, especially its higher echelon, has become a scapegoat for a bewildered public and power-hungry politicians. The confidence and security of the higher bureaucrats have been shaken to an extent hitherto unparalleled. This is due to devious and revengeful methods adopted by the politicians and political leaders in dealing with 'un-co-operative' officials. One of these ways is to transfer an officer for

11. Joseph LaPalombara, "Bureaucracy and Political Development: Notes, Queries and Dilemmas", *Bureaucracy and Political Development*, ed., Joseph LaPalombara, *op. cit.*, p. 54.

12. V.A. Pai Panandiker, "Values, Attitudes and Motivation of Civil Servants", *The Indian Journal of Public Administration*, Vol. XIII, No. 3, (July-September, 1966), p. 552.

offending a Minister or politician. Transfers could be made to less desirable places or posts or they could be so frequent as to completely ruin the personal finances of an officer. A ubiquitous misuse of the power of posting and transfer by political leaders has created an atmosphere in which equivocation, delay and avoidance of courageous and imaginative decisions become the safest course of action but which are not conducive to developmental work.

Our study also shows that the politicians tend to condemn and denounce the bureaucrats, and sometimes, publicly, whenever the members of the public register complaints against them.

We have seen in chapter five how the politicians pressurise the bureaucrats with various types of demands. Various group and organisations of society make all kinds of demands on the politicians. Although some amount of political pressure is inevitable in a democratic set up, excessive political pressures and influences not only paralyse the administration but also proves disadvantageous to people who do not have access to political leaders. Further, political pressures on appointment, promotion and transfer bring down the morale of the public servants and lead to frustration among them.

Political pressures put the bureaucrats on the horns of a dilemma, i.e., to choose between victimization and sacrificing the values of impartiality, independence and integrity. The best way the bureaucrats find to avoid victimization for non-compliance with political demands is either not to take any action or to push the matter upward in the hierarchy. Faced with political pressures, the bureaucrats also tend to take refuge in precedents and procedures. Thus, under political pressure, indecision, and inaction form the safest course for a peaceful, if not, a successful career to a bureaucrat.

Like the bureaucracy in other States and at the Centre, the Meghalayan bureaucracy also suffers from bureaucratic dysfunctions of corruption and inefficiency. Corruption and inefficiency are inter-related, and sometimes the one is found to be the cause of the other. Though a writer like Riggs[13] considers corruption to be concomitant of development, bureaucratic corruption in Meghalaya, as in the other third world countries, poses a challenge to the very viability of the system.[14] The bureaucratic dysfunctions of corruption and inefficiency cause great dissatisfaction and frustration among the people who, in turn, start questioning the very utility of our democratic set-up and administrative machinery. It is also not uncommon among the people to compare the standard of administrative efficiency and integrity during the British Rule with those of today and such comparison leads them to draw a gloomy picture of the present-day administrative scene in India. Bureaucratic corruption and inefficiency affect not only the day-to-day life of the citizen but also the future development of the nation.

> After all, the administration is the instrument of economic planning. If the tools are defective, the work is bound to be shoddy. Even if the development plans are well-conceived, a corrupt administration defeats their purpose and even leads them to disrupture.[15]

After discussing the role of bureaucracy as an institution in the development of the state, we shall now turn to a study

13. For details see Fred W. Riggs, *Administration in Developing Countries*, *op. cit.*

14. Referring to the wide-spread corruption in the state one M.L.A. said : "...corruption exists in our state and that is, the reason why developmental works cannot progress and there is not sign of clean administration ...if we give indulgence to such practice, I think it will take only a few more years that the people will rise against this government to tackle against the corruption which exists in the state of ours today". See *Meghalaya Legislative Assembly Debates*, Vol. 1, No. 2, (Budget Session, 1973), p. 29.

15. J.B. Kripalani, "Foreword" in S. Dwivedy and G.S. Bhargava's *Political Corruption in India*, (First. ed., New-Delhi : Popular Book Service, 1967), p. VIII.

of the role of bureaucrats as reflected in their values and attitudes. V.A. Pai Panandiker rightly observes :

> ...the character of all organisations is determined not so much by their structural systems but by the behaviour of their human element. At every stage and every point of the organisational operation, the values and attitudes which its personnel has, support of distort, build or undermine the organisational objectives; they determine the actual content of policy and shape the performance of the organisation. In other words, the behaviour of the administrative personnel can be functional or dysfunctional to the objectives of the organisation.[16]

Here, we shall study the value orientations of the bureaucrats towards the authoritatively-determined developmental goals. Such a study of the value-commitment of the bureaucrats is important because their awareness and commitment determine their behaviour and performance. Each actor in the decision-making process attaches his own meaning to the problems he confronts.[17] It is because of the importance of self-awareness and perception for developmental goals and values that a number of scholars have identified the development process as a state of mind, a tendency, a direction. As Kuldeep Mathur says :

> ... development involves a certain changes in the older order and more traditional value system. This change or stubborn to do so is reflected in the reactions of an individual in a developing society to an environment which is rapidly changing and is sometimes difficult to comprehend. But, in any concrete situation, in which an individual participates, he is faced with choices of alternative action. He evaluates these alternatives in his mind according to certain abstractions embodied in his past experience, some

16. V.A. Pai Panandiker, "Values, Attitudes and Motivation of the Civil Servants", *op. cit.*, p. 544.
17. Mathur, *op. cit.*, p. 11.

> political ideology or tradition. It is these assumptions that serve to attach meaning to all aspects of his environment. The objective validity of these perceptions is less significant than is the fact that they are believed to be true and present the realities of the situation from which emanates the bases of all action and reaction.[18]

Thus, the value-commitment of the bureaucrats in one of the most important factors in the development of the state.

For studying the politico-economic value orientations of the bureaucrats, we asked them twelve questions,[19] to elicit their views on four broad themes of democracy, equality, secularism and economic planning which together constitute the essence of political modernisation. An analysis[20] of the responses[21] shows that 61.82 percent of the bureaucrats believe in these four values and 34.54 percent do not believe, while 3.64 percent are found to be uncertain. Now, if we break up the responses value-wise, we find that the value of

18. *Ibid.*, p. 12. Joseph Spengler observes in this connection that, "the state of peoples politico-economic development together with its rate and direction, depends largely upon the content of the minds of its elites, which reflect in part, as do civilisations, the conceptions men form of the universe". See Bansal, *op. cit.*, p. 29.

19. For the questions, See Appendix C.

20. The responses we received were analysed in the form of a score table. For obtaining score results, numbers have been assigned to the replies. For instance, +1 indicates agreement, —1 indicates disagreement and **0** indicates uncertainty. Three questions were asked each on the themes of democracy, equality, secularism and economic planning and for obtaining score result the following method was followed : A believer on particular theme should score '−**2**' marks. That is a believer should disagree with two or more statement while, a non-believer should agree with two or more statements. The rest, i.e., those who agree with one question, disagree with other and is uncertain about a third is ranked in the category of uncertain.

21. For analysis of the responses, see Table 7 : 1.

democracy accounts for the largest number of believers (68.18 percent), followed by economic planning (65.45 percent), equality (59.09 percent) and secularism (54.54 percent), In the category of non-believer, the value of secularism accounts for the largest number of respondents (43.64 percent), followed by economic planning (34.55 percent), equality (31.82 percent) and democracy (28.18 percent). The value of equality accounts for the largest number of respondents in the category of uncertain (9.09 percent), followed by democracy (3.64 percent) and secularism (1.82 percent). Thus, on an average, the number of respondents who believe in these values is almost double the number of those who do not believe in these values.

Besides, the realisation of these developmental values and objectives, Meghalaya has certain goals of her own in the economic sphere which can be considered unique because of the geo-historical factors. The state being situated in a hilly terrain, bordering with Bangladesh lacks a well-developed transport and communication system which is a pre-condition of economic development. Besides transport and communication, other problem sectors in the state are agriculture, village development, border-areas development and industrialisation which have been given priority in the State's plan since the achievement of statehood. But what do the higher bureaucrats think about these programmes ?

To study the attitudes of the higher bureaucrats towards these programmes, we asked[22] them to identify the development programmes which they thought were most urgently required for the socio-economic development of the state and which development programmes they favoured least. An analysis[23] of the responses shows that the bureaucrats have preference for industrialisation and development of transport and communication over agriculture and other rural programmes. Industrialisation has been over-whelmingly

22. For the question, see Appendix C.
23. For the analysis, see Table 7 : 2.

mentioned by the bureaucrats as a means for the development of the state (32.47 percent of the responses), followed by development of transport and communication (12.99 percent of the responses). Although 44 bureaucrats in all consider the development programmes necessary, they do not favour all the programmes equally. This is evident from the table 7 : 3 which shows that agricultural and rural development programmes are favoured least by the bureaucrats followed by the programmes of village development and the development of areas.

The above findings of the present study are in sharp contrast to the developmental strategy of the state. This reveals the existence of a great hiatus between developmental planning and strategy and the priorities considered important by the implementing machinery. While top priority is given to agriculture and other rural development programmes in each plan, the higher bureaucracy does not appear to favour these programmes. This raises the question whether the higher bureaucracy has adequate involvement in the developmental programmes of the state when its members hold different priority sectors of development as important.

Bureaucracy has two elements : one is its structural-institutional element and the other is its behavioural element. In the preceding pages of this chapter we have seen how different structural-institutional elements of bureaucracy frustrate the goal of rapid development. Similarly, there exists a conflict between the behavioural elements of the bureaucracy and the developmental programmes of the government. Although a large number of bureaucrats are found to be in favour of the national values of democracy, secularism, equality and economic planning, with regard to the specific programmes of economic development of the state, the bureaucrats do not favour the priorities accorded to various sectors in the developmental programmes of the state.

The broad conclusion of this study is that the bureaucracy in Meghalaya is passing through a transitional and critical phase when it is not sufficiently equipped to act as a dynamic instrument of socio-economic change in the state. There exists a wide gap between role expectation and actual role performance of the higher bureaucracy. This gap is the result of the stresses and strains to which the bureaucracy is subjected both by its structural and institutional arrangements and behavioural patterns and value-orientations. The problems which the bureaucracy faces in Meghalaya are not unique to Meghalaya or India; they are common to all the developing countries. The developing countries are passing through a transitional phase in their development processes in which the traditional and modern structures, values and norms co-exist. Functioning in a predominantly traditional society, the bureaucracy is called upon to undertake massive tasks of modernisation and development. But as the bureaucracy is a sub-system of the social system, it possesses some of the particularistic characteristic of the traditional society. It is not suggested here that tradition and modernity are opposed to each other ; in fact, they possess a dialectical relationship and are complementary to each other. However, at the present stage of development, there is a conflict between tradition and modernity and it is this conflict which is at the heart of the problem of the ineffective role of bureaucracy in the development programmes in Meghalaya.

Appendices

Appendix-A

TABLE—1 : 1

IAS etc. Examinations

Condition of eligibility	*IAS*	*IFS*	*IPS*	*CS*
1. Age limits (years)	21 – 26	21 – 26	20 – 26	21 – 26
2. Minimum educational qualification	—	First Degree (any faculty)		—
3. Number of Permissible attempts	—	Not more than three chances for each category*		
Scheme of examination—written examination compulsory subjects – 3 (Genl. English-150, Genl. Knowledge-150, Essay-150 marks)	450	450	450	450
Optional subjects (each subject carries 200 marks)	3×200=600	3×200=600	2×200=400	3×200=600
Additional subjects (each subject carries 200 marks)	2×200=400	2×200=400	—	—

Personality Test	300	400	200	200
% of Personality Test to aggregate	17.14	21.62	19.04	16.00
Grand Total of Marks	1750	1850	1050	1250

*Category I—IAS and IFS.
Category II—IPS and Class II Police Service of Union Territories.
Category III—Central Services Class I and Class II.

Note : Each subject is covered in one paper. Optional subjects are of honours level, and additional subjects of masters level.

Source : Civil Services Examination, Report of the Committee on Recruitment Policy and Selection Method, Union Public Service Commission, 1976, p. 34.

TABLE—1 : 2*

Civil Service Examination : Conditions of Eligibility

(Following the Changes Introduced in 1979)

Age limit	*Minimum Educational Qualification*	*Number of Permissible attempts*	*Scheme of Examination*			
			Preliminary Examination		*Main Examination*	
			Subjects	*Marks*	*Subjects*	*Marks*
21 to 28 Years[a]	First Degree. (any faculty)	Three[b]	*Paper—I* General Studies	— 150	*Paper – I* One of the Indian languages included in the 8th schedule of the Constitution	300
			Paper—II Optional Subject	— 300	*Paper-II* English	300
					Paper-III & IV General Studies (300 marks in each paper)	600

* The table is prepared on the basis of data collected from an advertisement of Union Public Service Commission.

[a] The upper age limit is relaxable by three to eight years in case of different classes of candidates.

[b] The restriction on the number of attempt is not applicable in case of Scheduled Castes and Scheduled Tribes Candidates who are otherwise eligible.

		Paper-V, VI, VII & VIII Two optional subjects of two papers each (300 marks in each paper)	1200
		Interview	250
Total	450	Total	2650[d]

[c] The Paper I of the main examination on Indian language is not compulsory for candidates hailing from North-Eastern States/Union Territories of Arunachal Pradesh, Manipur, Meghalaya, Mizoram and Nagaland and also for candidates hailing from the state of Sikkim.

[d] The first and second paper of language and English being qualifying in nature, the marks obtained in these papers will not be counted for ranking. Therefore, the actual marks counted for ranking is (2650-600)=2050.

TABLE — 2 : 1

Distribution of State Government Employees

According to Caste/Tribe and Status as on (31st March, 1975)*

Castes/Tribes	*Gazetted*	*Non-Gazetted*	*Grade IV*	*Total*	*% to Total*
Scheduled Tribes (Hills)	415	6,233	2,692	9,340	56.41
Scheduled Tribes (Plains)	12	264	51	327	1.98
Scheduled Castes	20	570	194	784	4.74
Other Backward Classes	43	1,225	1,063	2,331	14.08
Others	299	2,352	1,123	3,774	22.79
Total	789	10,644	5,123	16,556	100.00

Source : ***Statistical Hand Book Meghalaya*, 1978.**
Directorate of Economics, Statistics and Evaluation, Government of Meghalaya, Shillong.

TABLE — 3 : 1

Age of Bureaucrats and Service

Service	*Age Group*				
	21 to 30	*31 to 40*	*41 to 50*	*51 to 60*	*Total*
IAS	1 (4.00)	9 (36.00)	10 (40.00)	5 (20.00)	25 (100.00)
ACS	—	4 (26.67)	7 (46.66)	4 (26.67)	15 (100.00)
MCS	5 (12.50)	24 (60.00)	8 (20.00)	3 (7.50)	40 (100.00)
MHS	—	4 (40.00)	4 (40.00)	2 (20.00)	10 (100.00)
MES	—	10 (50.00)	6 (30.00)	4 (20.00)	20 (100.00)
Total	6 (5.46)	51 (46.36)	35 (31.82)	18 (16.36)	110 (100.00)

TABLE — 3 : 2

Sex of Bureaucrats and Service

Service	*Male*	*Female*	*Total*
IAS	24 (96.00)	1 (4.00)	25 (100.00)
ACS	14 (93.33)	1 (6.67)	15 (100.00)
MCS	33 (82.50)	7 (17.50)	40 (100.00)
MHS	5 (50.00)	5 (50.00)	10 (100.00)
MES	20 (100.00)	—	20 (100.00)
Total	96 (87.27)	14 (12.73)	110 (100.00)

TABLE — 3 : 3

Provincial Background of Bureaucrats and Service

Service	*From within the state*	*From outside the state*	*Total*
IAS	14 (56.00)	11 (44.00)	25 (100.00)
ACS	12 (80.00)	3 (20.00)	15 (100.00)
MCS	38 (95.00)	2 (5.00)	40 (100.00)
MHS	4 (40.00)	6 (60.00)	10 (100.00)
MES	5 (25.00)	15 (75.00)	20 (100.00)
Total	73 (66.36)	37 (33.64)	110 (100.00)

TABLE — 3 : 4

Provincial Background of Bureaucrats and Specialisation

Specialisation	*From within the state*	*From outside the state*	*Total*
Non-technical	64 (80.00)	16 (20.00)	60 (100.00)
Technical	9 (30.00)	21 (70.00)	30 (100.00)

TABLE — 3 : 5

Rural/Urban Background of Bureaucrats and Service

Service	*Rural*	*Urban*	*Total*
IAS	4 (16.00)	21 (84.00)	25 (100.00)
ACS	4 (26.67)	11 (73.33)	15 (100.00)
MCS	14 (35.00)	26 (65.00)	40 (100.00)
MHS	1 (10.00)	9 (90.00)	10 (100.00)
MES	3 (15.00)	17 (85.00)	20 (100.00)
Total	26 (23.64)	84 (76.36)	110 (100.00)

TABLE — 3 : 6

Rural/Urban Background of Bureaucrats and Specialisation

Specialisation	*Rural*	*Urban*	*Total*
Non-technical	22 (27.50)	58 (72.50)	80 (100.00)
Technical	4 (13.33)	26 (86.67)	30 (100.00)

TABLE — 3 : 7

Religious Background of Bureaucrats and Service

Service	*Christian*	*Hindu*	*Sikh*	*Muslim*	*Total*
IAS	14 (56.00)	9 (36.00)	2 (8.00)	—	25 (100.00)
ACS	12 (80.00)	3 (20.00)	—	—	15 (100.00)
MCS	30 (75.00)	10 (25.00)	—	—	40 (100.00)
MHS	5 (50.00)	4 (40.00)	—	1 (10.00)	10 (100.00)
MES	5 (25.00)	14 (70.00)	—	1 (5.00)	20 (100.00)
Total	66 (60.00)	40 (36.36)	2 (1.82)	2 (1.82)	110 (100.00)

TABLE — 3 : 8

Religious Background of Bureaucrats and Specialisation

Specialisation	*Christian*	*Hindu*	*Sikh*	*Muslim*	*Total*
Non-technical	56 (70.00)	22 (27.50)	2 (2.50)	—	30 (100.00)
Technical	10 (33.33)	18 (60.00)	—	2 (6.67)	80 (100.00)

TABLE — 3 : 9

Caste Background of Bureaucrats and Service

Service	*Scheduled Tribes*	*General**	*Total*
IAS	15 (60.00)	10 (40.00)	25 (100.00)
ACS	12 (80.00)	3 (20.00)	15 (100.00)
MCS	33 (82.50)	7 (17.50)	40 (100.00)
MHS	6 (60.00)	4 (40.00)	10 (100.00)
MES	5 (25.00)	15 (75.00)	20 (100.00)
Total	71 (64.55)	39 (35.45)	110 (100.00)

* General Category includes bureaucrats belonging to categories other than Scheduled Castes and Scheduled Tribes.

TABLE — 3 : 10

Caste Background of Bureaucrats and Specialisation

Specialisation	*Scheduled Tribes*	*General**	*Total*
Non-technical	60 (75.00)	20 (25.00)	80 (100.00)
Technical	11 (36.67)	19 (63.33)	30 (100.00)

* General Category includes bureaucrats belonging to categories other than Scheduled Castes and Scheduled Tribes.

TABLE — 3 : 11

Father's Education of Bureaucrats and Service

Service	*Illiterate*	*Literate but no formal education*	*Non-Matric*	*Matriculate*	*Under Graduate*	*Graduate*	*Post* Graduate*	*N.R.*	*Total*
IAS	—	—	2 (8.00)	2 (8.00)	3 (12.00)	11 (44.00)	6 (24.00)	1 (4.00)	25 (100.00)
ACS	—	1 (6.67)	1 (6.67)	3 (20.00)	4 (26.67)	4 (26.67)	2 (13.33)	0 —	15 (100.00)
MCS	1 (2.50)	3 (7.50)	5 (12.50)	3 (7.50)	8 (20.00)	12 (30.00)	5 (12.50)	3 (7.50)	40 (100.00)
MHS	—	—	—	1 (10.00)	3 (30.00)	4 (40.00)	2 (20.00)	—	10 (100.00)
MES	—	1 (5.00)	—	3 (15.00)	5 (25.00)	7 (35.00)	3 (15.00)	1 (5.00)	20 (100.00)
Total	1 (0.91)	5 (4.55)	8 (7.27)	12 (10.91)	23 (20.91)	38 (34.54)	18 (16.36)	5 (4.55)	110 (100.00)

* The category of Post-Graduates includes all the degrees and diplomas which can be obtained only after Graduation.

TABLE — 3 : 12

Father's Education of Bureaucrats and Specialisation

Specialisation	*Illiterate*	*Literate but no formal education*	*Non-Matric*	*Matriculate*	*Under Graduate*	*Graduate*	*Post Graduate**	*N.R.*	*Total*
Non-technical	1 (1.25)	4 (5.00)	8 (10.00)	8 (10.00)	15 (18.75)	27 (33.75)	13 (16.25)	4 (5.00)	80 (100.00)
Technical	—	1 (3.33)	—	4 (13.33)	8 (26.67)	11 (36.67)	5 (16.67)	1 (3.33)	30 (100.00)

* The category of Post-Graduate includes all the degrees and diplomas which can be obtained only after Graduation.

TABLE – 3 : 13

Father's Occupation of Bureaucrats and Service

Service	*Agriculture*	*Business*	*Govt. Service*	*Profession*	*Teaching*	*N.R.*	*Total*
IAS	3 (12.00)	4 (16.00)	11 (44.00)	3 (12.00)	3 (12.00)	1 (4.00)	25 (100.00)
ACS	2 (13.33)	1 (6.67)	5 (33.33)	2 (13.33)	3 (20.00)	2 (13.33)	15 (100.00)
MCS	6 (15.00)	4 (10.00)	17 (42.50)	4 (10.00)	5 (12.50)	4 (10.00)	40 (100.00)
MHS	—	1 (10.00)	4 (40.00)	3 (30.00)	2 (20.00)	—	10 (100.00)
MES	2 (10.00)	1 (5.00)	10 (50.00)	3 (15.00)	3 (15.00)	1 (5.00)	20 (100.00)
Total	13 (11.82)	11 (10.00)	47 (42.73)	15 (13.64)	16 (14.54)	8 (7.27)	110 (100.00)

TABLE — 3 : 14

Father's Occupation of Bureaucrats and Specialisation

Specialisation	*Agriculture*	*Business*	*Govt. Service*	*Profession*	*Teaching*	*N.R.*	*Total*
Non-technical	11 (13.75)	9 (11.25)	33 (41.25)	9 (11.25)	11 (13.75)	7 (8.75)	80 (100.00)
Technical	2 (6.67)	2 (6.67)	14 (46.67)	6 (20.00)	5 (16.66)	1 (3.33)	30 (100.00)

TABLE — 3 : 15

Father's Annual Income of Bureaucrats and Service

Service	*Low* (*upto Rs. 5,000/-*)	*Middle* (*from Rs. 5,001/- to Rs. 10,000/-*)	*High* (*above Rs. 10,000/-*)	*N.R.*	*Total*
IAS	8 (32.00)	11 (44.00)	4 (16.00)	2 (8.00)	25 (100.00)
ACS	5 (33.33)	6 (40.00)	2 (13.33)	2 (13.33)	15 (100.00)
MCS	14 (35.00)	17 (42.50)	5 (12.50)	4 (10.00)	40 (100 00)
MHS	2 (20.00)	5 (50.00)	3 (30.00)	—	10 (100.00)
MES	5 (25.00)	9 (45.00)	5 (25.00)	1 (5.00)	20 (100.00)
Total	34 (30.91)	48 (43.63)	19 (17.27)	9 (8.18)	110 (100.00)

TABLE — 3 : 16

Father's Annual Income of Bureaucrats and Specialisation

Specialisation	*Low* (*upto Rs, 5,000/-*)	*Middle* (*from Rs. 5,001/- to Rs. 10,000/-*)	*High* (*above Rs. 10,000/-*)	*N.R.*	*Total*
Non-technical	27 (33.75)	34 (42.50)	11 (13.75)	8 (10.00)	80 (100.00)
Technical	7 (23.33)	14 (46.67)	8 (26.67)	1 (3.33)	30 (100.00)

TABLE — 3 : 17

Nature of Schooling of Bureaucrats and Service

Service	*English Medium*	*Vernacular*	*N.R.*	*Total*
IAS	17 (68.00)	8 (32.00)	—	25 (100.00)
ACS	8 (53.33)	6 (40.00)	1 (6.67)	15 (100.00)
MCS	21 (52.50)	17 (42.50)	2 (5.00)	40 (100 00)
MHS	6 (60.00)	4 (40.00)	—	10 (100.00)
MES	9 (45.00)	11 (55.00)	—	20 (100.00)
Total	61 (55.45)	46 (41.82)	3 (2.73)	110 (100.00)

TABLE — 3 : 18

Nature of Schooling of Bureaucrats and Specialisation

Specialisation	*English Medium*	*Vernacular*	*N.R.*	*Total*
Non-technical	46 (57.50)	31 (38.75)	3 (3.75)	80 (100.00)
Technical	15 (50.00)	15 (50.00)	—	30 (100.00)

TABLE — 3 : 19

Educational Qualification of Bureaucrats and Service

Service	*Under Graduate*	*Graduate*	*Post Graduate**	*N.R.*	*Total*
IAS	—	7 (28.00)	18 (72.00)	—	25 (100.00)
ACS	—	8 (53.33)	7 (46.67)	—	15 (100.00)
MCS	—	24 (60.00)	16 (40.00)	—	40 (100.00)
MHS	—	2 (20.00)	7 (70.00)	1 (10.00)	10 (100.00)
MES	3 (15.00)	12 (60.00)	4 (20.00)	1 (5.00)	20 (100.00)
Total	3 (2.73)	53 (48.18)	52 (47.27)	2 (1.82)	110 (100.00)

*The Category of Post-Graduate includes all the degrees and diplomas which can be obtained only after Graduation.

TABLE — 3 : 10

Educational Qualification of Bureaucrats and Specialisation

Specialisation	*Under Graduate*	*Graduate*	*Post Graduate**	*N.R.*	*Total*
Non-technical	—	39 (48.75)	41 (51.25)	—	80 (100.00)
Technical	3 (10.00)	14 (46.67)	11 (36.67)	2 (6.66)	30 (100.00)

*The Category of Post-Graduate includes all the degrees and diplomas which can be obtained only after Graduation.

TABLE — 4 : 1

Responses of Bureaucrats (According to Castes/Tribes) to The Statement that Officials from Outside the State do not Understand Local Problems and are not Interested in the Development of the State.

Castes/Tribes	*Agree*	*Disagree*	*N.R.*	*Total*
Scheduled Tribes	49 (69.01)	21 (29.58)	1 (1.41)	71 (100.00)
General*	18 (46.15)	19 (48.72)	2 (5.13)	39 (100.00)
Total	67 (60.91)	40 (36.36)	3 (2.73)	110 (100.00)

*General Category includes bureaucrats belonging to categories other than Scheduled Castes and Scheduled Tribes.

TABLE — 4 : 2

Motivation for Joining (According to Service)

Service	*Interested*	*No-alternative*	*Total*
IAS	17 (68.00)	8 (32.00)	25 (100.00)
ACS	8 (53.33)	7 (46.67)	15 (100.00)
MCS	18 (45.00)	22 (55.00)	40 (100.00)
MHS	5 (50.00)	5 (50.00)	10 (100.00)
MES	12 (60.00)	8 (40.00)	20 (100.00)
Total	60 (54.55)	50 (45.45)	110 (100.00)

TABLE — 4 : 3

Satisfaction with Nature of Work (According to Service)

Service	*Satisfied*	*Not-satisfied*	*Total*
IAS	19 (76.00)	6 (24.00)	25 (100.00)
ACS	9 (60.00)	6 (40.00)	15 (100.00)
MCS	22 (55.00)	18 (45.00)	40 (100.00)
MHS	4 (40.00)	6 (60.00)	10 (100.00)
MES	9 (45.00)	11 (55.C0)	20 (100.00)
Total	63 (57.27)	47 (42.73)	110 (100.00)

TABLE — 4 : 4

Satisfaction with Nature of Work
(According to Technical and Non-Technical Bureaucrats)

Specialisation	*Satisfied*	*Not-satisfied*	*Total*
Non-technical	50 (62.50)	30 (37.50)	80 (100.00)
Technical	13 (43.33)	17 (56.67)	30 (100.00)

TABLE—4 : 5

Satisfaction with Salary (According to Service)

Service	*Satisfied*	*Not-satisfied*	*Total*
IAS	9 (36.00)	16 (64.00)	25 (100.00)
ACS	5 (33.33)	10 (66.67)	15 (100.00)
MCS	12 (30.00)	28 (70.00)	40 (100.00)
MHS	2 (20.00)	8 (80.00)	10 (100.00)
MES	5 (25.00)	15 (75.00)	20 (100.00)
Total	33 (30.00)	77 (70.00)	110 (100.00)

TABLE—4 : 6

Satisfaction with Salary
(According to Technical and Non-technical Bureaucrats)

Specialisation	*Satisfied*	*Not-satisfied*	*Total*
Non-technical	26 (32.50)	54 (67.50)	80 (100.00)
Technical	7 (23.33)	23 (76.67)	30 (100.00)

TABLE—4 : 7

Satisfaction with Promotion
(According to Service)

Service	*Satisfied*	*Not-satisfied*	*Total*
IAS	15 (60.00)	10 (40.00)	25 (100.00)
ACS	6 (40.00)	9 (60.00)	15 (100.00)
MCS	12 (30.00)	28 (70.00)	40 (100.00)
MHS	5 (50.00)	5 (50.00)	10 (100.00)
MES	11 (55.00)	9 (45.00)	20 (100.00)
Total	49 (44.55)	61 (55.45)	110 (100.00)

TABLE—4 : 8

Satisfaction with Promotion
(According to Technical and Non-technical Bureaucrats)

Specialisation	*Satisfied*	*Not-satisfied*	*Total*
Non-technical	33 (41.25)	47 (58.75)	80 (100.00)
Technical	16 (53.33)	14 (46.67)	30 (100.00)

TABLE—4 : 9

Satisfaction with Prestige
(According to Service)

Service	*Satisfied*	*Not-satisfied*	*Total*
IAS	18 (72.00)	7 (28.00)	25 (100.00)
ACS	9 (60.00)	6 (40.00)	15 (100.00)
MCS	22 (55.00)	18 (45.00)	40 (100.00)
MHS	6 60.00)	4 (40.00)	10 (100.00)
MES	13 (65.00)	7 (35.00)	20 (100.00)
Total	68 (61.82)	42 (38.18)	110 (100.00)

TABLE—4 : 10

Satisfaction with Prestige
(According to Technical and Non-technical Bureaucrats)

Specialisation	*Satisfied*	*Not-satisfied*	*Total*
Non-technical	49 (61.25)	31 (38.75)	80 (100.00)
Technical	19 (63.33)	11 (36.67)	30 (100.00)

TABLE—5 : 1

Bureaucrats' Response to Frequency of Political Pressure (According to Service)

Service	*Very frequent*	*Frequent*	*Frequency less frequent*	*Least frequent*	*Never*	*Total*
IAS	9 (36.00)	8 (32.00)	5 (20.00)	3 (12.00)	—	25 (100.00)
ACS	6 (40.00)	5 (33.33)	2 (13.33)	2 (13.33)	—	15 (100.00)
MCS	13 (32.50)	17 (42.50)	6 (15.00)	4 (10.00)	—	40 (100.00)
MHS	3 (30.00)	2 (20.00)	3 (30.00)	2 (20.00)	—	10 (100.00)
MES	7 (35.00)	6 (30.00)	5 (25.00)	2 (10.00)	—	20 (100.00)
Total	38 (34.55)	38 (34.55)	21 (19.09)	13 (11.82)	—	110 (100.00)

TABLE—5 : 2

Nature of Political Pressure and Frequency

Nature of Political Pressure	*Very frequent*	*Frequent*	*Frequency*		*Never*	*N.R.*	*Total*
			Less frequent	*Least frequent*			
Demands concerning politician's personal interest and the interest of the members of the family	17 (15.45)	18 (16.36)	17 (15.45)	20 (18.18)	35 (31.82)	3 (2.73)	110 (100.00)
Demands concerning the interests of friends and relatives	22 (20.00)	22 (20.00)	20 (18.18)	18 (16.36)	25 (22.73)	3 (2.73)	110 (100.00)
Demands concerning the interests of supporters	33 (30.00)	35 (31.82)	18 (16 36)	13 (11.82)	8 (7.27)	3 (2.73)	110 (100.00)
Demands concerning the interests of the people of the Constituency	20 (18.18)	21 (19.09)	19 (17.27)	22 (20.00)	25 (22.73)	3 (2.73)	110 (100.00)

TABLE–5 : 3

Types of Political Pressure

Responses	*Number of responses given*	*Percentage of responses*
Making approach through Political Leaders at the higher level	100	38.17
Approach through Administrative Officers at the higher level	80	30.53
Persuasion through Administrator's friends and relatives	42	16.03
Promise of better career opportunities	16	6.11
Promise to take responsibility of consequences on himself	18	6.87
Pressure through demonstration like gheraos, dharnas, etc.	6	2.29
Total	262	100.00

Number of respondents in the sample 110

Non-respondents ... 3 (–)

107

Number giving 3 responses 60 $(60\times3)=180$

Number giving 2 responses 35 $(35\times2)=\ 70$

Number giving 1 response 12 $(12\times1)=\ 12$

Total number of responses =262

TABLE—5 : 4

Courses the Bureaucrats Follow to Deal with Political Pressure

Responses	*Number of responses given*	*Percentage of responses*
Express inability due to rules and regulations	75	27.98
Try to deal with the situation themselves but by seeking support from the higher level bureaucrats	64	23.88
Refer the case to higher ups	60	22.39
Try to deal with the situation themselves but by seeking support from the higher level political leaders	40	14.93
Deal with the situation themselves	12	4.48
Seek transfer to some other place	9	3.36
Appeal to the good sense of the politicians	8	2.98
Total	268	100.00

Number of respondents in the sample 110
Non-respondents ... 3 (—)

107

Number giving 3 responses	70	(70 × 3)	= 210
Number giving 2 responses	21	(21 × 2)	= 42
Number giving 1 response	16	(16 × 1)	= 16
Total number of responses			= 268

TABLE—5 : 5

Consequences of Non-compliance with Political Pressures

Responses	*Number of responses given*	*Percentage of responses*
Service condition is disturbed by transfer, complaint to higher authority	100	37.45
Cease to get any co-operation from the politicians	80	29.96
Service records spoiled	55	20.60
Public denigration or criticism	32	11.99
Total	267	100.00

Number of respondents in the sample	110
Non-respondent	3 (–)
	107

Number giving 3 responses	60	(60×3)	=180
Number giving 2 responses	40	(40×2)	= 80
Number giving 1 response	7	(7×1)	= 7
Total Number of responses			=267

TABLE—6 : 1

Responses of the Bureaucrats to the Question : 'What are the Different Types of Corruption Prevalent in Public Bureaucracy ?'

Responses	*Number of responses given*	*Percentage of responses*
Using official position for non-official purposes	64	26.02
Using government vehicles for personal use	56	22.76
Bribery	53	21.54
Showing favours to friends and relatives	38	15.45
Using official staff and stationery for personal use	35	14.23
Total	246	100.00

Number of respondents in the sample	110		
Non-respondents	3 (—)		
	107		
Number giving 3 responses	40	(40×3)	=120
Number giving 2 responses	58	(58×2)	=116
Number giving 1 response	10	(10×1)	= 10
Total number of responses			=246

TABLE—6 : 2

Responses of the Bureaucrats' to 'Factors Responsible for Corruption'

Responses	*Number of responses given*	*Percentage of responses*
Moral factor	80	34.78
Economic factor	70	30.43
Political factor	48	20.87
Structural factor	29	12.61
Cultural factor	3	1.30
Total	230	100.00

Number of respondents in the sample 110
Non-respondents ... 2 (–)

108

Number giving 3 responses 40 (40×3) =120
Number giving 2 responses 42 (42×2) = 84
Number giving 1 response 26 (26×1) = 26

Total number of responses =230

TABLE–6 : 3

Responses of the Bureaucrats to 'Remedial Measures for Removing Corruption'

Responses	*Number of responses given*	*Percentage of responses*
Societal	104	48.15
Economic	60	27.78
Political	27	12.50
Structural	25	11.57
Total	216	100.00

Number of respondents in the sample	110
Non-respondents	2 (–)
	108

Number giving 3 responses 34 (34×3)	=102
Number giving 2 responses 40 (40×2)	= 80
Number giving 1 response 34 (34×1)	= 34
Total number of responses	=216

TABLE—6 : 4

Responses of the Bureaucrats to 'Factors Responsible for Inefficiency'

Responses	*Number of responses given*	*Percentage of responses*
Administrative	65	24.25
Political	58	21.64
Social	56	20.90
Individual	50	18.66
Economic	39	14.55
Total	268	100.00

Number of respondents in the sample	110	
Non-respondents	2 (–)	
	108	

Number giving 3 responses	60 (60×3)	=180
Number giving 2 responses	40 (40×2)	= 80
Number giving 1 response	8 (8×1)	= 8
Total number of responses		=268

TABLE—6 : 5

Responses of the Bureaucrats to 'Measures for Removing Inefficiency'

Responses	*Number of responses given*	*Percentage of responses*
Administrative	96	36.50
Political	87	33.08
Individual	80	30.42
Total	263	100.00

Number of respondents in the sample 110
Non-respondents 2 (—)

108

Number giving 3 responses 56 (56 × 3) = 168
Number giving 2 responses 43 (43 × 2) = 86
Number giving 1 response 9 (9 × 1) = 9

Total number of responses = 263

TABLE—7 : 1

Value Commitment of the Bureaucrats

Values	*Commitment*			
	Believer	*Non-believer*	*Uncertain*	*Total*
Democracy	75 (68.18)	31 (28.18)	4 (3.64)	110 (100.00)
Equality	65 (59.09)	35 (31.82)	10 (9.09)	110 (100.00)
Secularism	60 (54.54)	48 (43.64)	2 (2.82)	110 (100.00)
Economic Planning	72 (65.45)	38 (34.55)	—	110 (100.00)
Total	272 (61.82)	152 (34.54)	16 (3.64)	440 (100.00)

TABLE—7 :2

Bureaucrats Response to the Question : 'Which Development Programmes do you think are Most Urgently Necessary ?'

Development Programmes	*Number of responses given*	*% of responses*
Agriculture : Foodgrain production, control of jhumming, development of cash crops, oil seeds, horticultural schemes	14	9.09
Development of transport and communications : Construction of roads and bridges	20	12.99
Village Programmes : Development of cottage industries, provision of drinking water, extension of educational benefits, rural electrification, tribal programmes, co-operative programmes	10	6.49
Development of border areas : Agriculture, animal husbandry, soil conservation, co-operation, education, roads, fisheries, transport subsidiary scheme, water supply, industries, handloom weaving, border areas marketing, strengthening of administrative machinery	16	10.39
Industrialisation	50	32.47

All the programmes are necessary	44	28.57
Total	154	100.00

Number of respondents in the sample	110
Non-respondents	3 (—)
	107

Number giving 2 responses 47 (47×2)	= 94
Number giving 1 response 60 (60×1)	= 60
Total number of responses	= 154

TABLE—7 : 3

Bureaucrat's Response to the Question 'Which Development Programmes do you Favour Least ?'

Development Programmes	*Number of responses given*	*% of responses*
Agriculture : Foodgrain production, control of jhumming, development of irrigation facilities, development of cash crops, oil seeds, horticultural schemes	45	32.61
Development of transport and communications : Construction of roads and bridges	3	2.17
Village Programmes : Development of cottage industries, provision of drinking water, extension of educational benefits, rural electrification, tribal programmes, co-operative programmes	20	14.49
Development of border areas : Agriculture, animal husbandry, soil conservation, cooperation, education, road, fisheries, transport subsidiary scheme, water supply, industries, handloom weaving, border areas marketing, strengthening of administrative machinery	34	24.64
Industrialisation	—	—

None of the Programme is of least importance	36	26.09
Total	138	100.00

Number of Respondents in the sample 110
Non-respondents 3 (—)

107

Number giving 2 responses	31 (31×2)	= 62
Number giving 1 response	76 (76×1)	= 76
Total number of responses		=138

APPENDIX B : CHARTS

CHART—4 : 1

Hierarchy in Public Bureaucracy (Non-technical) : Secretariat

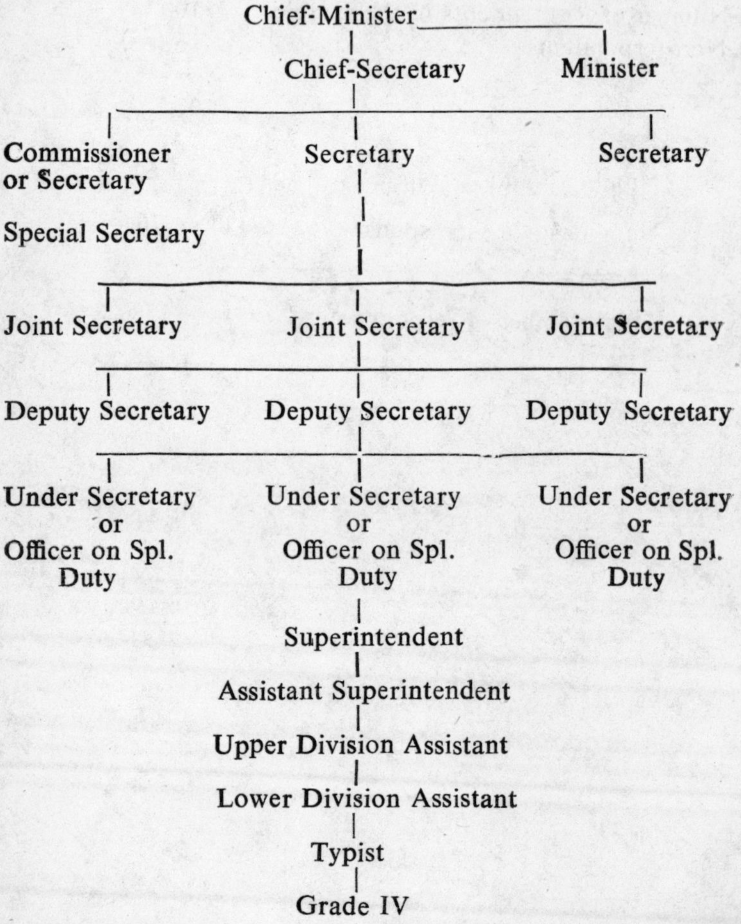

CHART—4 : 2

Hierarchy in Public Bureaucracy
(Technical Department) : P.W.D.

Chief-Engineer
&
Secretary
1
Additional Chief-Engineer
&
Additional Secretary
1
Deputy Chief-Engineer
&
Deputy Secretary

Superintending Engineer

Assistant Chief-Engineer
&
Under Secretary

Assistant Chief-Engineer
&
Under Secretary

Executive
Engineer

Sub-Divisional Officer/Assistant Engineer

Sub-Divisional
Officer

Sub-Engineer

Sub-Engineer

APPENDIX C

Questionnaire

Section—1

A-1. Age :

A-2. Place of birth : Please tick mark ( )
Village ( )
Town ( )
City ( )

A-3. State : ....

A-4. Caste/Tribe (Please also mention whether you belong to Scheduled Caste/Scheduled Tribe)
....

A-5. Religion : ....

A-6. Community : ....

A-7. Kindly give below information relating to your previous education and academic career—

	Name of the Institution	*Name of the Degree*	*Division/Grade*
a. School	....	....	....
	....	....	....
b. College	....	....	....
	....	....	....
c. University	....	....	....
	....	....	....

A-8. The Service to which you belong : ....

A-9. Entry into the Service was : Please tick mark ( )
Direct ( ) Promoted ( )

A-10. Did you serve anywhere before joining the present one : Yes/No. If yes, please indicate the nature of the job—

....

....

A-11. Education of your parents :

Father— Mother—

A-12. Father's profession and annual income :

....

Section—II

B-1. What are the existing principles, procedures and system of promotion ?

B-2. a. Are you satisfied with the present promotion system ? Yes/No.

b. Could you please explain ?

B-3. In case of promotion, what factors other than merit and seniority operate ?

B-4. Please give your suggestions for the improvement of the present system of promotion ?

B-5. Sometimes it is said that administrators at higher level in Meghalaya, being mostly drawn from outside the State, do not know the local problems and are not interested in development programmes of the State. What are your views on this statement ?

B-6. It is said that the I.A.S. officers live in ivory tower and look down the officers belonging to other services. Do you think this statement is true ?

B-7. Critics of Indian administration, say that it is dominated by the 'Generalists', who without enough technical knowledge, are placed at the head of technical departments which impedes the pace of development and undermines the initiative and enthusiasm of technical experts. Would you comment on this statement in the light of the conditions in Meghalaya ?

Section—III

C-1. Why did you choose your present career ? ....

....

....

C-2. Are you satisfied with the following aspects of your job ?

a. Nature of work in your present position Yes/No.

b. Salary that you receive Yes/No.

c. Method and chances of Promotion Yes/No.

d. Status and prestige that is associated with your job Yes/No.

Would you please explain why you say so ? ....

....

....

....

Section—IV

D-1. Speaking from your experience, how frequently do the politicians make unreasonable demands upon the administrators ? Please tick mark ( )

a. Very frequently ( )

b. Frequently ( )

c. Less frequently ( )

d. Least frequently ( )

e. Never ( )

D-2. Speaking from your experience, how frequently do the

politicians make demands of the following nature upon the bureaucrats ? Please tick mark ( )

	Very frequently (1)	*Frequently* (2)	*Less frequently* (3)	*Least frequently* (4)	*Never* (5)
a. Demands concerning politicians' personal interests and those of the members of his family	( )	( )	( )	( )	( )
b. Demands concerning the interests of the relatives and friends	( )	( )	( )	( )	( )
c. Demands concerning the interests of supporters	( )	( )	( )	( )	( )
d. Demands concerning the interests of the people of the constituency	( )	( )	( )	( )	( )
e. Any other	( )	( )	( )	( )	( )

D-3. Speaking from your experience, would you kindly suggest some important ways through which politicians exert pressure upon the administrators ?

D-4. When faced with the pressure from politicians to do something which is not proper, what courses are the administrators most likely to follow ? Please mention some important courses.

D-5. Speaking from your experience, would you kindly mention the possible consequences a bureaucrat has to face if he does not succumb to political pressure ?

Section—V

E-1. Would you kindly mention the important types of corruption that you consider to be prevalent in the public bureaucracy in Meghalaya ?

E-2. What do you think to be the most important causes of corruption in public bureaucracy in Meghalaya ? Could you kindly specify the causes.

E-3. Would you kindly suggest some important measures for removing corruption from the public bureaucracy ?

E-4. What do you think to be the important causes of inefficiency in the public bureaucracy in Meghalaya ? Would you please mention them ?

E-5. Would you kindly suggest from your experience some measures to be adopted for removing bureaucratic inefficiency ?

Section-VI

F-1. Some statements are given below. Please read them and tick mark ( ) against your response.

	Agree	Disagree	Do not know
i. Democracy in the present socio-economic condition of the country is harmful than advantageous	( )	( )	( )
ii. Election must be done away with for sometime	( )	( )	( )
iii. In fact what we probably need is a dictator for sometime	( )	( )	( )

iv. Certain communities have more talents	( )	( )	( )
v. Voting power to everybody has created problems	( )	( )	( )
vi. Women should have equal rights with men to reach the highest positions	( )	( )	( )
vii. The highest positions in the country should always belong to the majority community	( )	( )	( )
viii. Lack of respect for religion has led to present moral deterioration in our society	( )	( )	( )
ix. It is legitimate for a religious community to form a party to pursue its political interests	( )	( )	( )
x. All economic troubles of our nation have been caused by emphasis on socialism and public sector which have no incentive for economic investment and growth	( )	( )	( )
xi. If only we had accepted Gandhi's call of 'back to village', we would not have faced			

such a failure in economic development ( ) ( ) ( )

xii. The legitimate functions of government are law and order and not managing commercial and business activities ( ) ( ) ( )

F-2. Which of the following development programmes do you think are urgently necessary for the socio-economic development of the State ? Please tick mark ( )

a. Agriculture : Foodgrain production, control of jhumming, development of irrigation facilities, development of cash crops, oil seeds, horticultural schemes. ( )

b. Development of transport and communications : Construction of roads and bridges. ( )

c. Village programmes : Development of cottage industries, provision for drinking water, extension of educational benefits, rural electrification, tribal programmes, co-operative programmes. ( )

d. Development of border areas : Agriculture, animal husbandry, soil conservation, co-operation, education, roads, fisheries, transport subsidiary scheme, water supply, industries, handloom weaving, border areas marketing, strengthening of administrative machinery. ( )

e. Industrialisation. ( )

f. All the programmes are necessary. ( )

F-3. Which of the following development programmes do you favour least ? Please tick mark ( )

a. Agriculture : Foodgrain production, control of

jhumming, development of irrigation facilities, development of cash crops, oil seeds, horticultural schemes. ( )

b. Development of transport and communication : Construction of roads and bridges. ( )

c. Village programmes : Development of cottage industries, provision for drinking water, extension of educational benefits, rural electrification, tribal programmes, co-operative programmes. ( )

d. Development of border areas : Agriculture, animal husbandry, soil conservation, co-operation, education, roads, fisheries, transport subsidiary scheme, water supply, industries, handloom weaving, border areas marketing, strengthening, of administrative machinery. ( )

e. Industrialisation. ( )

f. None of the programmes is of least importance. ( )

APPENDIX A

Letter by Shri A.K. CHATTERJEE, I.A.S.*

From :

Shri A.K. Chatterjee,
General Manager,
Bihar State Road Transport Corporation,
PATNA.

To

The Chief Minister of Bihar,
PATNA.

Through proper channel.

Dear Sir,

I have learnt from the newspapers today that the Bihar Cabinet has decided to promote me to the super-time scale of the I.A.S. While I am grateful for the maganimity of your gesture, I regret it is rather difficult for me to accept the promotion for the following reasons :

For some time past, I have been feeling increasingly disillusioned about the utterly subservient role and insignificant authority of the public servant in the Government set-up of our State. An honest public servant has so little say in decision-making and in setting the course of administration that he is unable to contribute anything of lasting value to the larger interests of the people. Real authority has been highly concentrated in the hands of political functionaries and, in order to matter, a public servant has to seek proximity to this ultimate source of authority. Such proximity can usually be had only through dubious means which an honest and upright public servant cannot afford. Therefore, an honest and upright public servant inevitably finds himself largely irrelevant in the present set-up. He becomes a meaningless blob in a system based on favouritism and geared to serve the interests of political functionaries and their near and dear ones alone.

Unfortunately, a public servant is still important in the eyes of the people and they expect him to ensure justice, fair play, efficiency and service. But in the absence of required effective authority, he is unable to meet these expectations. This creates a hiatus between his supposed importance and his actual helplessness, between what people expect of him and what he is able to do, between his supposed role in the running of Government and the satisfaction he misses in his job. The higher he climbs the bureaucratic ladder, the wider becomes the gaps. For the climb raises people's expectations of him, but not his real status, discretion or authority which alone could improve his ability to contribute to the larger social cause.

The experience of this hiatus has of late caused me a considerable sense of humiliation and is affecting my idealism and zeal for work. And I am afraid this will get accentuated if I am sent further up the bureaucratic hierarchy through such a spurious elevation.

I, therefore, express my inability to accept the promotion to the Commissioner's grade in the I.A.S. I shall be grateful if you let me spend the rest of my service career with Government in my present grade and earn my bread without adding to my sense of mortification.

Yours faithfully,
Sd/-
(A.K. CHATTERJEE)

Copy forwarded to :

1. Chief Secretary,
   Govt. of Bihar, PATNA.
2. Commissioner-cum-Secretary,
   Personnel Deptt., Bihar, PATNA.
3. President/Secretary, I.C. and A.S.,
   Association, Bihar Branch, PATNA.

* Shri A.K. Chatterjee joined the Civil Service after topping the I.A.S. List in 1966. He has held important positions in the Government in Bihar State. Reproduced from "The Bureaucracy at the Crossroads" by Ajoy Bose, *The Hindustan Times*, New-Delhi, December 6, 1981.

Bibliography

Primary Source :

Administrative Reforms Commission Reports. New-Delhi : Government of India Press.

i. *Centre-State Relationships,* June,1969.

ii. *Delegation of Financial and Administrative Powers.* June, 1969.

iii. *Economic Administration,* July, 1968.

iv. *Machinery of the Government of India and its Procedure of Work,* Part I, March, 1967, and Part II, February, 1968.

v. *Machinery of Planning,* March, 1968.

vi. *Personnel Administration,* August, 1967.

Annual Report on the Working of the Meghalaya Public Service Commission for the year :

1972-73.

1973-74.

1974-75.

1975-76.

1976-77.

1977-78.

1978-79.

Ansari, *Assam and Meghalaya Pension Code with all Amendments and Short-notes*, Allahabad : Orient Law House, 1979.

Appleby, Paul H. *Public Administration in India : Report of a Survey*, Delhi : Cabinet Secretariat, Organisation and Method Division, Government of India, 1953.

————*Re-examination of India's Administrative System with Special Reference to Administration of Governments Industrial and Commercial Enterprise*, New-Delhi : Cabinet Secretariat, Organisation and Method Division, Government of India.

Census of India, 1971, District Census Handbook, U.K. and J. Hills District, Series 13, Part-XA & B, Shillong : Directorate of Census Operations, Meghalaya.

Census of India, 1971, Meghalaya Series 13, Part IIA, Shillong: Directorate of Census Operations, Meghalaya.

Civil Service Examination : Report of the Committee on Recruitment Policy and Selection Methods. New-Delhi : Union Public Service Commission, 1976.

Delegation of Financial Rules, 1960, Shillong : Assam Government Press, 1961.

Dewan, V.K. *The Travelling Allowance Rules with Amendments of Assam and Meghalaya*, Allahabad : Orient Law House, 1978.

————*Fundamental Rules and Subsidiary Rules* (Assam and Meghalaya), Second Revised ed., Allahabad : Orient Law House, 1979.

Draft Annual Plan, 1975-76, Shillong : Planning Department, Government of Meghalaya, 1974.

Draft Annual Plan, 1976-77, Shillong : Planning Department, Government of Meghalaya.

Draft Annual Plan, 1977-78, Shillong : Planning Department, Government of Meghalaya.

Draft Annual Plan, 1978-79, Shillong : Planning Department, Government of Meghalaya, 1977.

Employment News (Special Supplement), 20th December, 1980.

Fifth Five-Year Plan : *Draft Proposal*, Vol.I, Shillong : Planning Department, Government of Meghalaya, 1973.

Gorwala, A.D. *Report on Public Administration*, Planning Commission, Government of India, 1951.

Handbook of General Circulars, Director, Organisation and Method Division, Government of Assam, 1965.

Khongwir, S.D. Deputy Chief-Minister, *Review of the Implementation of Development Schemes and Programmes for 1978-79* : *A Supplement to the Budget Speech 1978-79*, Shillong : Government of Meghalaya, 1978.

Meghalaya Civil Service Rules, Shillong : Government of Meghalaya, 1975.

Meghalaya Legislative Assembly Debates :
(April Session, 1970).
(Budget Session, 1970).

Meghalaya Legislative Assembly Debates :
(Budget Session, 1971).
(March Session, 1971).
(Winter Session, 1971).

Meghalaya Legislative Assembly Debates :
(Budget Session, 1972).
(March/April Session, 1972).
(June/July Session, 1972).
(Winter Session, 1972).

Meghalaya Legislative Assembly Debates :
(Budget Session, 1973).
(Emergent Session, 1973).
(March Session, 1973).
(Winter Session, 1973).

Meghalaya Legislative Assembly Debates :
(Budget Session, 1974).
(March Session, 1974).
(March/April Session, 1974).
(June/July Session, 1974).
(Winter Session, 1974).

Meghalaya Legislative Assembly Debates :
(Budget Session, 1975).
(Winter Session, 1975).

Meghalaya Legislative Assembly Debates :
(Budget Session, 1976).
Winter Session, 1976).

Meghalaya Legislative Assembly Debates :
(Vote-on-Account Session, 1977).
(Budget Session, 1977).
(Winter Session, 1977).

Meghalaya Legislative Assembly Debates :
(Vote-on-Account Session, 1978).
(Budget Session, 1978).

Meghalaya Transfer of Land (Regulation) Act, 1971, Government of Meghalaya.

Memorandum Submitted to the Chief Secretary, Government of Meghalaya by Meghalaya Civil Service Officers' Association, 19th March, 1979 (unpublished).

Mid-Term Review of Fifth Five Year Plan : Revised Outlays and Targets, Shillong : Planning Department, Government of Meghalaya, 1976.

Public Accounts Committee Report for the year 1970-71 to 1974-1975 (Government of Meghalaya).

Report of the Committee on Prevention of Corruption, Delhi : Ministry of Home Affairs, Government of India, 1964.

Report of the Meghalaya Pay Commission, 1979, Shillong : Meghalaya Government Press.

Rules of Executive Business, Shillong : Cabinet Affairs and Personnel Department, Government of Meghalaya, 1972.

Statistical Handbook, Meghalaya, Shillong : Directorate of Economics, Statistics and Evaluation, Government of Meghalaya, 1978.

Secondary Sources :

Books :

Abedin, N. *Local Administration and Politics in Modernising Societies* : Bangladesh and Pakistan, First ed., Dacca : National Institute of Public Administration, 1973.

Albrow, M. *Bureaucracy*, London : Macmillan, 1970.

Anon, "Transfer of the Collector Matsyapura", *New Challenges in Administration,* ed. Committee on Case Studies, New-Delhi : Indian Institute of Public Administration, 1972.

Appleby, Paul H. *Public Administration for a Welfare State*, Bombay : Asia Publishing House, 1970.

Arora, R.K. *Comparative Public Administration* : *An Ecological Perspectives*, New-Delhi : Associated Publishing House, (N.D.).

Avasthi, A. "The Challenge of Administrative Change in India", *Administrative Change in India*, ed. Ramesh K. Arora, Jaipur : Aalekh Publishers (N.D.).

Bansal, P.L. *Administrative Development in India*, First ed., New-Delhi : Sterling Publishers Pvt. Ltd., 1974.

Barkataki, S. *Tribes of Assam*, New-Delhi : National Book Trust of India, 1969.

Barnard, C.I., *The Functions of the Executive*, Cambridge : Massachusetts, Harvard University Press, 1951.

Bendix, R. *Nation-Building and Citizenship* : *Studies of Our Changing Social Order*, New-Delhi : Wiley Eastern Pvt. Ltd., 1969.

Bhalerao, C.N. *Public Service Commissions of India : A Study*, First. ed., New-Delhi : Sterling Publishers Pvt. Ltd., 1966.

———"Bureaucracy as an Institution of Modernisation : Some Issues", *Administrative Change in India*, ed. Ramesh K. Arora, Jaipur : Aalekh Publishers (N.D.).

Bhambhri, C.P. *Bureaucracy and Politics in India*, First ed., Delhi : Vikas Publications, 1971.

———*Administrators in a Changing Society*, First ed., Delhi ; National Publishing House, 1972.

Bhargava, G.S. *India's Watergate : A Study of Political Corruption in India*, First ed., Delhi : Arnold Heinemann Publishers, 1974.

Blau, P.M. *The Dynamics of Bureaucracy : A Study of Interpersonal Relations in Two Government Agencies*, Chicago : The Chicago University Press, 1963.

Braibanti, R. "Public Bureaucracy and Judiciary in Pakistan", *Bureaucracy and Political Development*, ed., Joseph LaPalombara, Princeton, New-Jersey : Princeton University Press, 1967.

Chanda, A. *Indian Administration*, Second ed., London : George Allen and Unwin Ltd., 1967.

Cozier, M. *The Bureaucratic Phenomenon*, New-Delhi : Eurasia Publishing House, 1975.

Dalton, E.T. *Tribal History of North-East India*, Delhi : Cosmo Publications, 1973.

Dubin, R. *Human Relations in Administration*, Third ed., New-Delhi : Prentice Hall of India Pvt. Ltd., 1970.

Dutt, D. "In Politics" *Corruption in India*, ed. Suresh Kohli, First ed., New-Delhi : Chetna Publications, 1975.

Dwivedy, S. and G.S. Bhargava, *Political Corruption in India*, First ed., New-Delhi : Popular Book Service, 1967.

Eisentadt, S.N. "Bureaucracy and Political Development", *Bureaucracy and Political Development*, ed. Joseph LaPalombara, Princeton, New-Jersey : Princeton University Press, 1967.

Eldersveld, S-J., A.P. Barnabas and V. Jagannadham, *The Citizen and the Administrator in a Developing Democracy : an Empirical Study in Delhi State*, New-Delhi : India Institute of Public Administration, 1968.

Franda, M.F. "Administration and Politics in West Bengal", *Administration, Politics and Development in India*, ed. C.N. Bhalerao, First ed., Bombay : Lalvani Publishing House, 1972.

Gadgil, D.R. "Planning and Administration", *Administration, Politics and Development in India*, ed. C.N. Bhalerao, First ed., Bombay : Lalvani Publishing House, 1972.

Gerth, H.H. and C.W. Mills (eds.) *From Max Weber Essays in Sociology*, London : Routledge and Kegan Paul Ltd., 1974.

Goodnow, H.F. *The Civil Service of Pakistan : Bureaucracy in a New Nation*, New-Haven : Yale University Press, C. 1964.

Gupta, B.B. *Problems of Indian Administration*, Allahabad : Chugh Publications, 1975.

Hall, R.H. *Organisations : Structure and Process*, Englewood Cliffs, New-Jersey : Prentice-Hall Inc., C. 1972.

Heady, F. *Public Administration : A Comparative Perspective*, Englewood, New-Jersey : Prentice-Hall Inc., 1979.

Hoselitz, B.F. "Levels of Economic Performance and Bureaucratic Structures", *Bureaucracy and Political Development*, ed. Joseph LaPalombara, Princeton, New-Jersey : Princeton University Press, 1967.

Iengar, H.V.R. *Administration in India : A Historical Review*, First ed., Bombay : Bharatiya Vidya Bhavan, 1967.

Jagannadham, V. "Social Administration in India", *Administrative Change in India,* ed. Ramesh K. Arora, Jaipur: Aalekh Publishers (N.D.).

Katz D. and Robert L. Kahn, *The Social Psychology of Organisations,* New-Delhi : Wiley Eastern Pvt. Ltd., 1970.

Khan, A.R. *Ozaratir Du Bachhar* (Two Years of Ministry), Dacca : Naoroj Kitabistan, 1972.

Khosla, G.D. "Corruption Down the Ages", *Corruption in India,* ed. Suresh Kohli, First ed., New-Delhi : Chetna Publications, 1975.

Kothari, R. *Politics in India,* New-Delhi : Orient Longman Ltd., 1972.

———"Forword" *Administrative Change in India,* ed. Ramesh K. Arora, Jaipur : Aalekh Publishers (N.D.).

Kothari S. and Ramashray Roy, *Relations Between Politicians and Administrators at the District Level,* First ed., New-Delhi : Indian Institute of Public Administration and the Centre of Applied Politics, 1969.

Kripalani, J.B. "Foreword", *Political Corruption in India,* S. Dwivedy and G.S. Bhargava, First ed., New-Delhi : Popular Book Service, 1967.

LaPalombara, J. "An Overview", *Bureaucracy and Political Development,* ed. Joseph LaPalombara, Princeton University Press, 1967.

———"Bureaucracy and Political Development : Notes, Queries and Dilemmas", *Bureaucracy and Political Development,* ed. Joseph LaPalombara, Princeton, New-Jersey : Princeton University Press, 1967.

Mathur, K. *Bureaucratic Responses to Development,* First ed., Delhi : National Publishing House, 1972.

Mathur, K. and Mohit Bhattacharya, *Administrative Response to Emergency,* First ed., Delhi : Concept Publishing Co., 1975.

Mehta, B. *Dynamics of State Administration*, First ed., Allahabad : Chugh Publications, 1975.

Merton, R.K. "Bureaucratic Structure and Personality" in *Social Theory and Social Structure*, New-Delhi : Amerind Publishing Co. Pvt. Ltd., 1975.

Mishra, B.B. *Bureaucracy in India : A Historical Analysis of Development upto 1947*, First ed., Bombay : Oxford University Press, 1977.

Monteiro, J.B. *Corruption : Control of Maladministration*, First ed., Bombay : Manaktalas, 1966.

Morris-Jones, W.H. *The Government and Politics of India*, Bombay : B.I. Publications, 1974.

Mudaliar, N.M. "Incentive in Public Service", *Administration and Politics in Modern Democracies*, ed., Sardar Patel Institute of Administration, Madras, Allahabad : Chugh Publications, 1976.

Myrdal, G. *Asian Drama : An Inquiry into the Poverty of Nations*, Vol. II, London : Allen Lane, The Penguine Press, 1968.

Narain, I. and P.C. Mathur, "Politics and Federalism in India: A Developmental Hypothesis—The Case of Rajasthan", *Administration, Politics and Development in India*, ed. C.N. Bhalerao, First ed., Bombay : Lalvani Publishing House, 1972.

Nayar, P.K.B. *Leadership, Bureaucracy and Planning in India : A Sociological Study*, First ed., New-Delhi : Associated Publishing House, 1969.

Prasad, A. *The Block Development Officer : A Portrait of Bureaucracy in India*, First ed., Patna : Associated Book Agency, 1976.

Prasad, A.D. *Corruption and Administration*, Patna : Basant Publications (N.D.).

Prasad, B. *The Indian Administarative Service*, New-Delhi : S. Chand & Co., 1968.

Prasad, G.K. *Bureaucracy in India : A Sociological Study*, First ed., New Delhi : Sterling Publishers Pvt. Ltd., 1974.

Presthus, R. *The Organisational Society : An Analysis and a Theory*, New-York : Random House Inc., 1962.

Pye, L.W. "Administration, Politics and Development in New States", *Administration, Politics and Development in India*, ed., C.N. Bhalerao, First. ed., Bombay : Lalvani Publishing House, 1972.

Rao, P.V.R. *Red Tape and White Cap*, First ed., New-Delhi : Orient Longmans Ltd., 1970.

Rao, V.V.A. *A Century of Tribal Politics in North-East India 1874-1974*, Delhi : S. Chand & Co. Ltd., 1976.

Riggs, F.W., *Administration in Developing Countries : The Theory of Prismatic Society*, Boston : Houghton Muffin Company, 1964.

———"Bureaucrats and Political Development : A Paradoxical View", *Bureaucracy and Political Development*, ed. Joseph LaPalombara, Princeton, New-Jersey : Princeton University Press, 1967.

Roy, R. *Bureaucracy and Development : The Case Study of Indian Agriculture*, First ed., New-Delhi : Manas, 1975.

Singhi, N.K. *Bureaucracy : Positions and Persons*, First ed., New-Delhi : Abhinav Publications, 1974.

Spangenberg, B. *British Bureaucracy in India : Status, Policy and the I.C.S., in the Late 19th Century*, First ed., New-Delhi : Manohar, 1976.

Spengler, J.J. "Bureaucracy and Economic Development", *Bureaucracy and Political Development*, ed., Joseph LaPalombara, Princeton, New-Jersey : Princeton University Press, 1967.

Srinivas, M.N. *Caste in Modern India*, Bombay : Asia Publishing House, 1977.

Subramaniam, V. *Social Background of India's Administrators*, New-Delhi : Publication Division, Ministry of Information and Broadcasting, Government of India, 1971.

Suleiman, E. N. *Politics, Power and Bureaucracy in France : The Administrative Elite*, Princeton, New-Jersey : Princeton University Press, C. 1974.

Tannenbaum, A.S. *Social Psychology of the Work Organisation*, London : Tavistock Publications Ltd., 1971.

Taub, R.P. *Bureaucrats under Stress : Administrators and Administration in an Indian State*, Calcutta : Firma K.L. Mukhopadhyay, 1969.

Tyagi, A.R. *The Civil Service in a Developing Society*, First ed., Delhi : Sterling Publishers Pvt. Ltd., 1969.

Vaish, R.P. *Reorientation in Administrative Strategy and Planning*, New-Delhi : S. Chand & Co., 1970.

Zimba, D.T. *Geography of Meghalaya*, Shillong : Lama Villa (N.D.).

Periodicals and Newspapers :

Adiseshiah, W.T.V. "Psychological Criteria for Administrative Service", *The Indian Journal of Public Administration*, Vol. VII, No. 2, (April-June,1961), pp. 158-169.

Aiyar, S.P. "Political Context of Indian Administration", *The Indian Journal of Public Administration*, Vol. XVII, No.3, (July-September, 1971), pp. 337-354.

Appleby, Paul H. "History and Precedent Vs. Reform", *The Indian Journal of Public Administration*, Vol. 1, No. 4, (October-December, 1955), pp. 303-309.

——— "Concerning Ministers", *The Indian Journal of Public Administration*, Vol. 1, No. 2, (April-June, 1955), pp. 89-91.

Assam Tribune (Gauhati), 1970-1980.

Attlee, C.R. "Civil Servants, Ministers, Parliament and the

Public", *The Indian Journal of Public Administration*, Vol .1 No. 2, (April-June, 1955), pp. 95-103.

Banerji, S. "A Unified Civil Service ?" *The Indian Journal of Public Administration*, Vol. IX, No. 2, (April-June, 1963), pp. 189-211.

Barve, S.G. "The Larger Political Context of Administrative Reforms", *The Indian Journal of Public Administration*, Vol. XII, No. 3, (July-September, 1966), pp. 352-355.

Bayley, D.H. "The Effect of Corruption in a Developing Nation", *The Western Political Science Quarterly*, Vol. XIX, No. 4, (December, 1966), pp. 719-732.

———- "The Policy of Preventive Detention 1950-63", *The Indian Journal of Public Administration*, Vol. X, No. 2, (April-June, 1964), pp. 235-256.

Bhalerao, C.N. "Changing Pattern of Development Administration in the Districts", *The Indian Journal of Public Administration*, Vol. XII, No. 1, (January-March, 1966), pp. 123-131.

Bhambhri, C.P. "A Study of Relationship Between Prime Minister and Bureaucracy in India", *The Indian Journal of Public Administration*, Vol. XVII, No. 3, (July-September, 1971),pp. 367-382.

Butani, K.N. "Leadership in Administration", *The Indian Journal of Public Administration*, Vol. II, No. 4, (October-December, 1956), pp. 325-328.

Chaturvedi, M.K. "Commitment in Civil Service", *The Indian Journal of Public Administration*, Vol. XVII, No. 1, (January-March, 1971), pp. 40-46.

Chowdhry, K. "Developing Administrators for Tomorrow", *The Indian Journal of Public Administration*, Vol. XV, No. 2, (April-June, 1969), pp. 221-227.

"Corruption : Third Time Lucky", *Economic and Political Weekly*, Vol. XIII, No. 40, (October 7, 1978), pp. 1683-1684.

Dey, B.K. "Bureaucracy and Development: Some Reflections", *The Indian Journal of Public Administration*, Vol. XV, No. 2, (April-June, 1969), pp. 228-248.

Dube, S.C. "Bureaucracy and Economic Development", *The Indian Journal of Public Administration*, Vol. XII, No. 3, (July-September, 1966), pp. 343-351.

Dubhashi, P.R. "Committed Bureaucracy", *The Indian Journal of Public Administration*, Vol. XVII, No. 1, (January-March, 1971), pp. 33-39.

——— "Satisfaction of an Administrative Career", *The Indian Journal of Public Administration*, Vol. XV, No. 1, (January-March, 1969), pp. 110-117.

Editorial, *Anandabazar Patrika*, (Calcutta, November 21, 1978).

Eldersveld, S.J. "Bureaucratic Contact with the Public in India". *The Indian Journal of Public Administration*, Vol. XI, No. 2, (April-June, 1965), pp. 216-235.

Gadgil, N.V., "Accountability of Administration", *The Indian Journal of Public Administration*, Vol. 1, No. 3, (July-September, 1955), pp. 193-203.

Goswami, U.L. "The Structure of Development Administration", *The Indian Journal of Public Administration*, Vol. 1, No. 2, (April-June, 1955), pp. 110-118.

Hajjar. S.G. "Towards Understanding the Concept of Bureaucratic Rationality", *The Indian Journal of Public Administration*, Vol. XIV, No. 2, (April-June, 1973), pp. 148-162.

Implanter, (Shillong) 1973-1979.

Iyer, R.R. "Understanding Our Bureaucracy", *The Indian Journal of Public Administration*, Vol. XII, No. 4, (October-December, 1966), pp. 697-716.

Jagannadham, V. "Administration and the Citizen", *The Indian Journal of Public Administration*, Vol. XVII, No. 4, (October-December, 1971), pp. 601-616.

———— "Review of Developments in Social Administration in India", *The Indian Journal of Public Administration*, Vol. IX, No. 3, (July-September, 1963), pp. 425-440.

Jha, L.K. "Mr. Red Tape", *The Indian Journal of Public Administration*, Vol. XI, No. 4, (October-December, 1965), pp. 680-682.

Khosla, J.N. "Development Administration : New Dimensions", *The Indian Journal of Public Administration*, Vol. XIII, No. 1, (January-March, 1967), pp. 16-31.

Khosla R.P. "Training the Administrator : The Problem of Motivation", *The Indian Journal of Public Administration*", Vol. XI, No. 4, (October-December, 1965), pp. 721-730.

———— "Bureaucrats : The Loss of Vision", *The Indian Journal of Public Administration*, Vol. XI, No. 1, (January-March, 1965), pp. 35-41.

Long, N. E. "Bureaucracy and Constitutionalism", *The American Political Science Review*, Vol. XLVI, No. 3, (September, 1952), pp. 808-818.

Maheshwari, S. "The Specialist and the Generalist in Public Administration", *The Indian Journal of Public Administration*, Vol. XXI, No. 1, (January-March, 1975).

———— "Training in Public Administration in India", *The Indian Journal of Public Administration*, Vol. XVII, No. 4, (October-December, 1971), pp. 617-633.

Mathai, J. "Administration : Then and Now", *The Indian Journal of Public Administration*, Vol. V, No. 1, (January-March, 1959), pp. 8-18.

Mehta, A. "Administrative Leadership", *The Indian Journal of Public Administration*, Vol. XI, No. 4, (October-December, 1965), pp. 671-679.

Mehta, B. " Some Thoughts on State Administration", *The Indian Journal of Public Administration*, Vol. IX, No. 2, (April-June, 1963), pp. 174-181.

Morale in the Public Services (Report of a Conference, January 3-4, 1959), New-Delhi : Indian Institute of Public Administration, August, 1959.

Nye, J.S. "Corruption and Political Development : A Cost Benefit Analysis", *The American Political Science Review*, Vol. LXI, No. 2, (June, 1967), pp. 417-427.

Panandiker, V.A.P. and S.S. Kshirsagar, "A Profile of Development Bureaucracy in India", *The Indian Journal of Public Administration*, Vol. XVIII, No. 4, (October-December, 1972), pp. 505-532.

—— "Bureaucracy in India : An Empirical Study", *The Indian Journal of Public Administration*, Vol. XVII, No. 2, (April-June, 1971), pp. 187-208.

Panandiker, V.A.P. "Development Administration : An Approach", *The Indian Journal of Public Administration*, Vol. X, No. 1, (January-March, 1964), pp. 34-43.

—— "Values, Attitudes and Motivation of Civil Servants", *The Indian Journal of Public Administration*, Vol. XII, No. 3, (July-September, 1966), pp. 544-558.

Paranjape, H. K. "Political and Administrative Problems of Implementing the Indian Plan", *The Indian Journal of Public Administration*, Vol. IX, No. 4, (October-December, 1963), pp. 608-648.

Patel, H.M. The Civil Servants and the Public", *The Indian Journal of Public Administration*, Vol. VI, No. 2, (April-June 1960), pp. 125-130.

"Political Vs. Bureaucratic Power", *Economic and Political Weekly*, Vol. XII, No. 41, (October 8, 1977), p. 1730.

Prakash, K. "The Annual Assessment and Promotion System in Indian Bureaucracy", *The Indian Journal of Public Administration*, Vol. XII, No. 4, (October-December, 1966), pp. 770-809.

Rai, H. "The Changing Role of District Officer (1860-1960)",

The Indian Journal of Public Administration, Vol. IX, No. 2, (April-June,1963), pp. 238-257.

———— "Paternalism in Indian Administration : The Non-Regulation System of Field Administration under the British", *The Indian Journal of Public Administration*, Vol. XV, No. 2, (April-June, 1969), pp. 193-211.

Rai, H. and S.K. Singh, "Indian Bureaucracy : A Case of Representativeness", *The Indian Journal of Public Administration*, Vol. XIX, No. 1. (January-March, 1973), pp. 1-15.

Rieger, H.C. "Bureaucracy and the Implementation of Economic Plan in India", *The Indian Journal of Public Administration*, Vol. XIII, No. 1, (January-March, 1967), pp. 32-42.

Santhanam, K. "Financial Discipline for Union and State Governments", *The Indian Journal of Public Administration*, Vol. XII, No. 3, (July-September, 1966), pp. 499-503.

Sayre, W.S. "Some Problems of Public Administration in a Developing Economy", *The Indian Journal of Public Administration*, Vol. VIII, No. 2, (April-June, 1962), pp. 137-152.

Sivaraman, B. Generalist and the Specialists in Administration", *The Indian Journal of Public Administration*, Vol. XVII, No. 3, (July-September, 1971), pp. 383-396.

Snowiss, L.M. "The Education and Role of the Superior Civil Service in India", *The Indian Journal of Public Administration*, Vol. VII, No. 1, (January-March, 1961), pp. 6-25.

Statesman, (Calcutta), 1970-1980.

Subramaniam, V. "Role of Civil Service in Indian Political System", *The Indian Journal of Public Administration*, Vol. XVII, No. 2, (April-June, 1971), pp. 238-264.

————"The Indian Administrative Tradition : Myth and Reality", *The Indian Journal of Public Administration*, Vol. XIII, No. 2, (April-June, 1967), pp. 217-226.

Zahedi, S. "Corruption in Developing Countries : The Iranian Case", *Administrative Change*, Vol. V, No. 2, (January-June, 1978), pp. 141-150.

Election Manifestoes :

Election Manifesto of the AU Party Hill Leaders Conference (APHLC), 1977 and 1978.

Election Manifesto of the Congress, 1977 and 1978.

Election Manifesto of the Hill State Peoples Democratic Party (HSPDP), 1977 and 1978.

Name Index

Subject Index